The
BEACHCOMBER'S GUIDE
to
SEASHORE LIFE
in the
PACIFIC NORTHWEST

The
BEACHCOMBER'S
GUIDE
to
SEASHORE LIFE
in the
PACIFIC NORTHWEST

J. DUANE SEPT

HARBOUR PUBLISHING

HARBOUR PUBLISHING
P.O. Box 219
Madeira Park, BC Canada
V0N 2H0
www.harbourpublishing.com

Cover photos and all other photos in this book by the author
Cover design, page design and composition by Martin Nichols, Lionheart Graphics
Printed and bound in Canada

Harbour Publishing acknowledges financial support from the Government of Canada through the Book Publishing Industry Development Program and the Canada Council for the Arts, and from the Province of British Columbia through the British Columbia Arts Council and the Book Publisher's Tax Credit through the Ministry of Provincial Revenue.

THE CANADA COUNCIL | LE CONSEIL DES ARTS
FOR THE ARTS | DU CANADA
SINCE 1957 | DEPUIS 1957

BRITISH
COLUMBIA
ARTS COUNCIL
Supported by the Province of British Columbia

Canadian Cataloguing in Publication Data

Sept, J. Duane, 1950–
    The beachcomber's guide to seashore life

Includes index.
ISBN 1-55017-204-2

1. Seashore biology—Northwest, Pacific. I. Title.
QH104.5.N6S46 1999   578.769'9'09795   C99-910316-4

*To my wife Sue and my children
Christy and Dusty
for their encouragement
and support*

Contents

Plants

Introduction

The Pacific Northwest coast is one of the world's richest, most diverse habitats for intertidal marine life. Hundreds of species and subspecies of animals and plants live along these shores, and each of them has developed a unique niche in which it lives, coexisting with its neighbors. To learn what these species are and how they are inter-related is a step toward learning how all the parts of the world work together in the giant puzzle we call life.

The intertidal zone—that part of the shoreline that is submerged in water at high tide and exposed at low tide—is a particularly gratifying place to observe wildlife and plant life alike. Species are diverse, abundant and endlessly interesting, and many of them can be observed easily without any special knowledge or equipment. Some are animals that are found both intertidally and subtidally, but whose appearance is completely transformed out of water. Anemones, for instance (see pp. 33–41), are often seen on the beach with their tentacles closed, and some marine worms (pp. 43–52) close their tentacles or leave distinctive signs on a beach when the tide recedes. Other species, such as the moonglow anemone (p. 34) or Merten's chiton (p. 58), occur in several color forms.

This guide is designed to enhance your experience of observing and identifying animal and plant species in the many fascinating intertidal sites of the Pacific Northwest. Many of these areas are so rugged they seem indestructible, but in fact they are fragile ecosystems, affected by every visit from man. Please tread carefully, exercise caution (see pp. 18–19) and let your eyes, camera and magnifying glass be your main tools for exploring the seashore.

Understanding Tides

Tides are caused primarily by the gravitational forces of both the moon and the sun upon the earth. These gravitational forces override the centrifugal forces of the earth's rotation. They create a high tide, or "bulge" (see figure below) of water on the earth near the moon, which has a stronger gravitational effect than the sun because it is so much closer to the earth. A similar "bulge" is created on the opposite side of the earth. When the tide is high in one area, the displacement of water causes a low tide in another area. The earth makes one complete revolution under the "bulges" during one tide cycle, so there are two high tides and two low tides during each tide cycle. Tides have the greatest range when the moon is closest to earth.

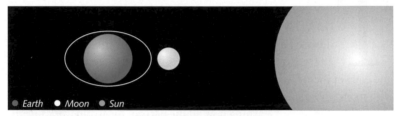

Earth ● Moon ● Sun

Figure 1

Earth ● Moon ● Sun

Figure 2

During the new moon, the combined gravitational pull of the sun and the moon generate even higher tides and correspondingly lower tides (see Figure 1). During the full moon, however, the moon's and sun's gravitational pull oppose each other (Figure 2), which dampens the tidal effect. The lunar cycle is completed every 27$\frac{1}{3}$ days, thus the moon orbits earth 13 times each year.

On each day of the year there are two high tides and two lows. The best time to view intertidal creatures is close to the lowest tide, so plan to arrive an hour or two before low tide. You can find this time—as well as the predicted height of the tide—by checking tide tables, available from tourist,

Low and high tide from the same location.

sporting goods and marine supply stores and often published in local newspapers. (Keep in mind that these tables are usually based on standard time and on a particular geographical reference point, so daylight savings time and your actual location may have to be factored in.)

Tidal heights are measured from different reference points in the USA and Canada. For the most accurate information, use the reference point closest to the area you plan to visit. In the USA, tides of 0.0' are the average of the lower low tides for that year. Tides lower than this value are referred to as minus tides in the USA. In Canada, the published tide tables are 2.5' (.8 m) lower than equivalent values in the USA. Times when tide levels are lower than 0.0' in the USA and 2.5' (.8 m) in Canada are excellent for observing animal and plant life at intertidal sites. Any visit will be rewarding, but these are the optimum times to see intertidal life.

Understanding Intertidal Habitats

The rich marine life found "at the edge" of the Pacific Ocean is due in part to the wide variety of habitats in this range. Some creatures occupy quite a limited habitat, hardly venturing from a small area throughout most of their adult lives, because they can tolerate a very narrow range of conditions. Other more adaptable species can be seen in several intertidal zones and into the ocean depths.

The intertidal region comprises several different habitats and zones. Each combination provides a unique set of physical conditions in which many creatures survive and coexist.

These two shorelines are very different, but they illustrate that intertidal species have preferred habitats (intertidal zones) regardless of the type of shoreline.

An intertidal zone is characterized by several "key" species of marine flora and fauna—species typically found within that zone. The zone may be only a favored location; the species may occur in other zones as well.

SAND BEACHES AND MUD FLATS

We often picture the Pacific coast as a vast sandy beach with gentle waves rolling toward shore, but this is only one of the many environments where seashore creatures have survived for centuries.

Thousands of years have passed since the last glaciers left their enormous deposits of sand and clay. Through time, the movement of land and sea have shifted huge volumes of these materials, which have provided numerous intertidal creatures with a place to burrow. The presence of many of these animals can be detected only by a slight dimple or irregularity in the surface of the sand or mud.

SAND BEACHES

This sandy beach is the home to the bay ghost shrimp (p. 112).

Sand beaches are commonly found in both exposed and protected sites. Exposed sandy areas occur as sandspits or sand beaches. Creatures commonly seen on such beaches include the Pacific razor-clam (p. 93) and purple olive (p. 77). These and other species are well adapted to survive the surf-pounded beach. Protected beaches or sand flats, away from the pounding surf, are a significantly different habitat, often occupied by Dungeness crab (p. 121), Nuttall's cockle (p. 91) and other species that are not adapted to the pounding waves of the outer coast. Some species occur in both exposed and protected sand beach habitats.

MUD FLATS

This mud beach is home to several worms and clams.

Mud flats are situated in sheltered locations such as bays and estuaries. Like sandy shores, they support a smaller variety of obvious intertidal life than rocky shorelines do. The yellow shore crab (p. 123) and Pacific gaper (p. 92) are species to look for in these areas.

Several species are characteristic of both mud flats and sand beaches. These include Lewis's moonsnail (p. 72), Pacific geoduck (p. 99) and soft-shell-clam (p. 98).

ROCKY SHORES

Rocky shores occur in a wide variety of forms. These rocks move little from year to year.

This boulder area provides a habitat for a wide variety of life forms.

Creatures have evolved special adaptations to live in certain habitats, so different species are found on exposed rocky shores than on sheltered ones. The California mussel (p. 85) and black Katy chiton (p. 61) occur in exposed areas, whereas more sheltered rocky sites harbor such creatures as the painted anemone (p. 39) and hairy hermit (p. 117).

Marine biologists divide rocky shores, as all shorelines, into several distinct intertidal zones: the splash zone and the high, middle and low intertidal zones. On rocky shores these zones are especially evident. The placement of these creatures in the various zones is likely a complex combination of adaptations and environmental factors, including heat tolerance, food availability, shelter and suitable substrate availability. The presence of predators may also limit the range of intertidal zones an animal can inhabit. Purple stars (p. 135), for example, prey upon the California mussel (p. 85), which pushes the mussel into a higher intertidal habitat.

SPLASH ZONE
This zone can be easily overlooked as an intertidal zone, and the few small species present here seem to occur haphazardly. But these creatures are actually out of the water more than they are in it, so they must be quite hardy to tolerate salt, heat and extended dry periods. The acorn barnacle (p. 105) and ribbed limpet (p. 65) are two of these species.

HIGH INTERTIDAL ZONE
This zone is characterized by such species as the mask limpet (p. 66), giant green anemone (p. 36) and California mussel (p. 85). Nail brush seaweed (p. 171) is one plant species that occurs in this zone, typically on top of rocks. (Seaweed species, like invertebrates, live in specific areas of the intertidal habitat.)

MIDDLE INTERTIDAL ZONE

This zone, also called the mid-intertidal zone, is home to the Vosnesensky's isopod (p. 108) and plate limpet (p. 64), as well as feather boa kelp (p. 164) and rockweed (p. 166). Most creatures in the mid-intertidal zone are normally not found in subtidal waters.

LOW INTERTIDAL ZONE

The sunflower star (p. 135) and purple sea urchin (p. 138) are among the many creatures to be found in the low intertidal zone, site of the most diverse and abundant marine life in the entire intertidal area. Creatures here often are found in subtidal waters too. In the low intertidal zone there is more food, shelter and probably a greater chance that the animal will be caught in a very low tide, as low tides affect this zone only rarely during the year compared with the high and mid-intertidal zones. The time marine life is exposed to the heat of the sun is also reduced; as a result heat is not a major limiting factor on the creatures of the low intertidal zone. There are also more species to be found in subtidal waters.

MICRO HABITATS

UNDER ROCKS

This environment is an important one. Whether the shore is rock, gravel, sand or mud, many species such as the daisy brittle star (p. 136), purple shore crab (p. 123) and black prickleback (p. 151) require this micro habitat for survival.

TIDEPOOLS

The grainyhand hermit (p. 116), aggregating anemone (p. 35), mossy chiton (p. 56), stout shrimp (p. 110), umbrella crab (p. 112) and many other species are often found in tidepools but are not restricted to them. These creatures live in a somewhat sheltered environment that may be different from the zone in which the pool is located.

FLOATING DOCKS AND PILINGS

These man-made sites attract a wide range of marine plants and invertebrates. Like rocky shores, they provide solid places for settling. The plumose anemone (p. 40), giant barnacle (p. 105) and shield-backed kelp crab (p. 119) commonly invade this habitat. Some are often attached to or living on the floating dock, so viewing is not restricted to low tides.

Harvesting Shellfish

One of the great pleasures of beachwalking can be gathering shellfish for a fresh dinner of seafood. Be aware that you need a licence to harvest seashore life such as clams, oysters and (in some areas) seaweeds, and there are harvesting seasons and bag limits. Before you take any shellfish, check with local officials for current restrictions.

Shellfish harvest areas may also be closed due to pollution, or to harmful algal blooms such as red tides (see below). Check with local authorities to make sure the area you wish to harvest is safe. Then let the fun begin!

RED TIDE

At certain times of the year, tiny algae reproduce rapidly in what is referred to as an algal bloom. Each of these algae can contain minute amounts of toxins, which are then concentrated in the body tissues of filter-feeding animals such as oysters, clams, mussels, scallops and other shellfish. Once the bloom dies, the animals' bodies begin to cleanse themselves of the toxins naturally, a process that takes time—as little as four to six weeks, but as long as two years for species such as butter clams.

Some experts believe that harmful algal blooms can produce a poison (saxitoxin) that is 10,000 times more toxic than cyanide. So if you eat even a tiny amount of shellfish that have ingested these toxins, you can become seriously or even fatally ill with paralytic shellfish poisoning (PSP). Symptoms include difficulty in breathing, numbness of tongue and lips, tingling in fingertips and extremities, diarrhea, nausea, vomiting, abdominal pain, cramps and chills. Reports of this ailment go as far back as human occupation along the Pacific Northwest coast.

Authorities regularly monitor shellfish for toxin levels, and affected areas are closed to shellfish harvesting. Watch for local postings of closures on public beaches and marinas, but to make sure, check with a PSP hotline or ask fisheries officials before harvesting any shellfish.

PSP (RED TIDE) HOTLINES
To obtain current marine toxin information contact the following:
British Columbia: Fisheries and Oceans,
24-hour recorded message, (604) 666-2828.
Washington: Washington Department of Health,
PSP Hotline, (800) 562-5632.
Oregon: Oregon Department of Agriculture,
Shellfish Safety Hotline, (503) 986-4728.

Protecting Our Marine Resource

Today more than ever it is essential for us to take responsibility for protecting our natural surroundings, including our marine environments. At many coastal sites human presence is becoming greater—sometimes too great. Habitat destruction, mostly from trampling, has been severe enough to cause authorities to close some intertidal areas to the public. In most cases this is not willful damage but people's unawareness of how harmful it can be simply to move around a seashore habitat.

To walk safely through an intertidal area, choose carefully where to step and where not to step. Sand and rock are always the best surfaces to walk on, when they are available. Mussels have strong shells which can often withstand the weight of a man without difficulty. Barnacles can also provide a secure, rough walking surface and can quickly recolonize an area if they become dislodged.

Please return all rocks carefully to their original positions, taking care not to leave the underside of any rock exposed. Take all containers back with you when you leave, as well as any debris from your visit. And please leave your dog at home when you visit intertidal sites.

Observing Intertidal Life

A magnifying glass is a must for any visit to the seashore, and a camera is the best way to take souvenirs. Another excellent item to take along is a clear plastic jar or plastic pail. Fill it with cool salt water and replace the water frequently. This will enable you to observe your finds for a short time with minimal injury to them. Make sure to return them to the exact spot where you found them. And if you must handle sea creatures, do so with damp hands so their protective slime coatings will not be harmed.

A Note of Caution

Before you visit an intertidal site, be aware of tide times and plan accordingly. During any visit to the beach it is important to stay out of low-lying areas which have no exit, and to keep a close watch on the water at all times. Many an unsuspecting beachcomber has become stranded on temporary islands formed by the incoming tide.

Strong wave action can take you by surprise. Dangerous waves come by a number of different names—sneaker waves, rogue waves, etc.—all of which indicate the nature of waves in exposed situations. Unexpected and powerful waves can and do take beach visitors from the shore. If you do get caught off guard by a wave, the best defense is to lie flat, grabbing onto any available rocks that may provide a handhold. This will make it possible for the wave to roll over you rather than taking you out to sea. A vigorous surf can also toss logs up on shore unexpectedly. Please be careful!

Seaweeds can present a slippery obstacle to those venturing into intertidal areas. In order to provide food and protection for the many creatures found along the shore, these plants cover just about everything. In some areas a two-footed and two-handed approach is necessary to move around safely. Rubber boots with a good tread will help you observe intertidal life without slipping or getting soaked. It's a good idea to exercise caution around barnacles and such creatures, as their shells are hard and sharp-edged.

Even for a short visit, take along a backpack, some drinking water and a small first aid kit.

Visiting the intertidal sites of the Pacific Northwest is one of the most rewarding pastimes on earth. A little bit of preparation and a healthy dose of caution will help make every trip to the seashore a wonderful adventure.

Getting the Most Out of This Guide

The field guide section of this book (pp. 21-183) includes colour photographs of the common animals and plants to be seen along the Pacific Northwest seashore, and concise information that will help you identify species.

Name: The current or most useful common name for the species; also the scientific name, a Latin name by which the species is known all over the world. This scientific name has two parts: the genus (a grouping of species with common characteristics) and the species.

Other names: Any other common or scientific names known for the species.

Description: Distinguishing physical features, behavior and/or habitat to aid in identifying the species.

Size: Dimension(s) of the largest individuals commonly seen.

Habitat: The type of area where the species lives (see Understanding Intertidal Habitats, pp. 12–16).

Range: The area of the Pacific Northwest where the species is found.

Notes: Other information of interest, usually relating to the natural history of the species or ways in which it differs from a similar species.

Animals

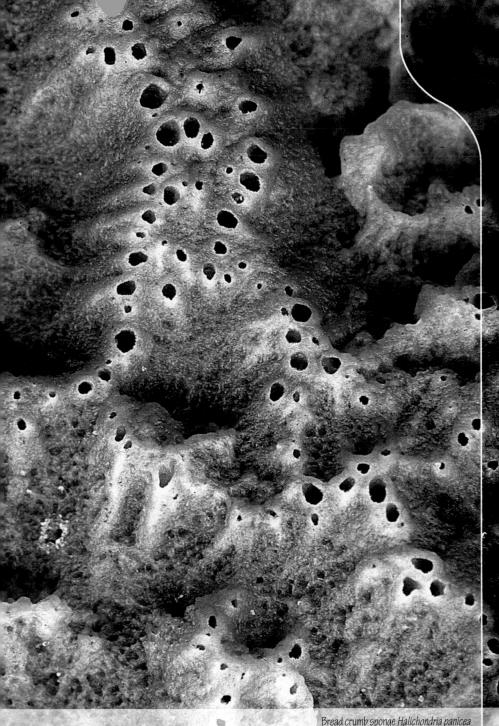

Bread crumb sponge *Halichondria panicea*

SPONGES
Phylum Porifera

Sponges are filter-feeding, colonial animals which live together as a larger unit. They appear to be plants, but are in fact invertebrate animals. Unique to the animal world, sponges have canals throughout their bodies which open to the surrounding water, allowing both oxygen and food particles to reach each sponge.

⟩BREAD CRUMB SPONGE

Halichondria panicea

Other name: Crumb of bread sponge.
Description: Soft, encrusting or crust-like sponge varying in color from yellow to light green. Several volcano-shaped pores (oscula) on surface.
Size: To 2" (5.1 cm) thick.
Habitat: Low intertidal zone to subtidal depths of 200' (60 m).
Range: Alaska to southern California.
Notes: Species gets its name from bread crumb-like texture. If broken, it is said to smell like gunpowder after being ignited. Various nudibranchs feed on this sponge, including the Monterey dorid (see p. 81), which can often be found on the sponge once the tide has receded.

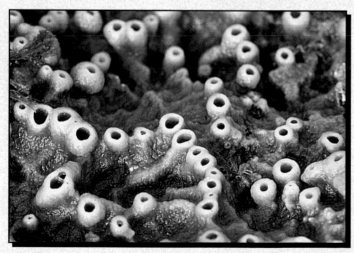

▷ RED ENCRUSTING SPONGE

Ophlitaspongia pennata
(and others)

Other names: Red sponge; scarlet sponge; velvety red sponge.

Description: Bright red to red-orange with tiny, closely spaced star-like pores (oscula). Surface is velvety to touch.

Size: To 39" (1 m) in diameter, 1/4" (6 mm) thick.

Habitat: On overhanging rocks and shady crevices, mid-intertidal zone to subtidal water 10' (3 m) deep.

Range: Southern BC to California.

Notes: Most common of several species of sponges which look very similar to this species. A microscope is required to tell them apart. Check specimen closely to find the red nudibranch (see p. 81) which perfectly matches the sponge in color. The nudibranch also lays its red eggs on this sponge, its main food source.

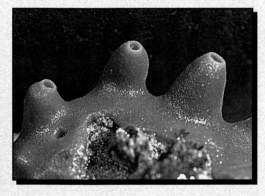

▷ PURPLE ENCRUSTING SPONGE

Haliclona permollis

Other names: Purple sponge; violet volcano sponge; encrusting sponge.

Description: Soft and encrusting or flat and crust-like sponge varying in color from pink to purple. Volcano-shaped pores (oscula) on surface.

Size: To 36" (91 cm) across, 1⁵/8" (4.1 cm) thick, but normally much smaller.

Habitat: On rocks and floating docks and in tidepools, mid-intertidal zone to subtidal water 20' (6 m) deep.

Range: BC to central California.

Notes: Several nudibranchs feed on this beautiful sponge. The ringed nudibranch (see p. 82) is able to find this sponge by chemicals which the sponge releases into the water.

Aggregating anemone
Anthopleura elegantissima

HYDROIDS, JELLIES, SEA ANEMONES, COMB JELLIES
Phyla Cnidaria & Ctenophora

The phylum Cnidaria includes hydroids, scyphozoan (bell-shaped) jellies, sea anemones and corals. This group has somewhat specialized organs for digesting or stinging. Many species have alternating generations from attached to free-swimming stages.

Comb jellies (phylum Ctenophora) are transparent like true jellies, but shaped much differently. These remarkable organisms are spherical or flattened into a ribbon shape, and they move by cilia or small hairs arranged in rows. Eggs and sperm are released from the mouth into the water, where they develop into small versions of the adult. There is no alternation of generations as there is in the bell-shaped jellies.

Phylum Cnidaria

Hydroids • Class Hydrozoa

› PURPLE ENCRUSTING HYDROCORAL
Allopora sp.

Other names: Purple stylasterine; purple carpet; formerly *Stylantheca* sp.
Description: An encrusting colony, vivid purple in color, covered in minute pits. Touching the surface reveals its **hard texture**.
Size: To 6" (15 cm) across, 1/8" (3 mm) thick.
Habitat: Low intertidal zone and below in exposed areas, often on faces of shaded rocks. Found at the lowest of tides in areas of extreme tidal fluctuations.
Range: BC to central California.
Notes: A somewhat uncommon hydrocoral. Purple encrusting sponge (see p. 25) is similar looking, with a noticeably soft texture and large openings rather than tiny pores.

›WINE-GLASS HYDROID
Obelia sp.

Other name: Sea plume.
Description: White in color. Individual main stems hold many smaller branches, giving an overall bushy look.
Size: To 10" (25 cm) tall.
Habitat: Colonies are found attached to floats, large seaweeds or rock in shallow tidepools, low intertidal zone to water 165' (50 m) deep.
Range: Alaska to southern California.
Notes: The wonderful name of this hydroid is very descriptive of the tiny coverings to the animal's feeding portions, but a microscope is necessary to see these wine glasses and make positive identification.

›TURGID GARLAND HYDROID
Sertularella turgida

Description: Displays elongated yellow stalks with distinctive wavy pattern.
Size: 2" (5 cm) high, 1½" (4 cm) wide.
Habitat: Low intertidal zone to water 528' (160 m) deep.
Range: BC to San Diego, California.
Notes: Very little is known about the biology of this distinctive hydroid. We do know that to reproduce, it retains its eggs while sperm are released to the sea for fertilization.

>Ostrich-plume Hydroid

Aglaophenia sp.

Description: Elongated feather-like plumes attached to rock, varying in color from yellow to light red or black.
Size: To 5" (13 cm) high.
Habitat: In surf-swept rock clefts on exposed shores, intertidal to water 528' (160 m) deep.
Range: Alaska to San Diego, California.
Notes: This species is easily confused with a plant, but hydroids start out as larvae called planula, and as adults are composed of tiny filter-feeding polyps. The elongated yellow eggs are often found attached to the plumes.

>Water Jelly

Aequorea sp.

Other names: Many-ribbed hydromedusa; many-ribbed jellyfish; water jellyfish; *Aequorea aequorea; Aequorea victoria.*
Description: Transparent bell-shaped jelly with 100 or more rib-like radial canals and trailing tentacles.
Size: To 3" (8 cm) in diameter.
Habitat: In open water and close to shore.
Range: Alaska to California.
Notes: Various species of water jellies are found world-wide. Their luminescence is easily observed at night as soft, circular balls of pulsing light. This species is known to eat other species of jellies and on occasion to cannibalize its own species.

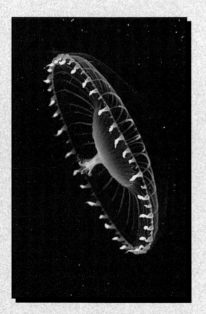

> AGGREGATING JELLY

Eutonina indicans

Description: Transparent umbrella with short tentacles. 4 radial canals are visible in the umbrella. The central peduncle hangs below the umbrella edge.
Size: To 1³/₈" (3.5 cm) in diameter.
Habitat: In sheltered areas near surface.
Range: Bering Sea to Santa Barbara, California.
Notes: Most often observed in large numbers from spring to fall. It feeds on a variety of small invertebrate eggs and larvae.

Bell-shaped Jellies • Class Scyphozoa

The rhythmic pulses of jellies are intriguing to observe—indeed, their fluid movements have a near-hypnotic effect. The purpose of this movement is probably to keep the animal near the surface of the water. Its seemingly random wanderings are influenced and aided by water currents.

Jellies date back to Precambrian times: one Australian fossil has been aged at 750 million years. There are a thousand known species of these primitive carnivores, which feed primarily on zooplankton. The life cycle of a jelly has distinct stages which include either a polyp (a tube-like organism with a mouth and tentacles to capture prey) or a medusa (umbrella-shaped organism) stage. The jelly captures its food, then lifts it to its mouth to eat.

Jellies are composed of as much as 96 percent water, but several species are consumed as food in various Pacific cultures. They are eaten boiled, dried or raw. The giant sunfish *Mola mola*, which has been known to grow to 2,700 lbs (1,215 kg), attains its huge size by feeding on jellies and similar coelenterates with nibbling and sucking techniques. This fish has been seen as far north as the Queen Charlotte Islands.

>LION'S MANE
Cyanea capillata

Other names: Sea blubber; sea nettle.
Description: Bell-shaped with smooth, near-flat top; shaggy clusters on ventral side with trailing tentacles. Yellow-brown to orange.
Size: Normally to 20" (50 cm) in diameter, tentacles to 10' (3 m) long; with one report of tentacles to 119' (36 m) long.
Habitat: Usually found floating near surface, occasionally stranded on the beach.
Range: Alaska to southern California.
Notes: The largest jelly in the world. Its tentacles deliver a burning sensation and rash to those who touch it. **Exercise caution**, even if you find a jelly stranded on the beach. All jellies are poisonous to some degree, and human reactions to the toxins vary from a mild rash to blistering and even, occasionally, death.

Species feeds on small fish, crustaceans and other animals it comes into contact with. Some species of fish find the lower portion of the bell provides refuge from their enemies.

Floating on water surface.

Stranded on shore.

❯ MOON JELLY
Aurelia labiata

Other names: Moon jellyfish; white sea jelly.
Description: Translucent, bell-shaped, with many short trailing tentacles and 4 round or horseshoe-shaped gonads or reproductive organs. Color whitish—often with a touch of pink, purple or yellow.
Size: 4–16" (10–40 cm) in diameter, 3" (7.5 cm) high.
Habitat: Usually found floating near surface.
Range: Alaska to southern California.
Notes: Sometimes collects in quiet waters such as harbors when plankton blooms in the spring. In these large aggregations, spawning also occurs. Tentacles cause a slight rash when handled. When the sun is visible, this jelly uses it as a compass to migrate in a southeasterly direction.
The moon jelly is often misidentified as *Aurelia aurita*, a European species now also found in California.

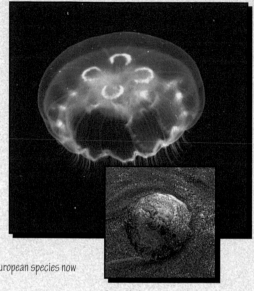

Stranded on shore.

COMB JELLIES
Phylum Ctenophora

 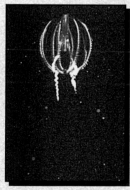

With extended tentacles.

With retracted tentacles.

❯ SEA GOOSEBERRY
Pleurobrachia bachei

Other names: Comb jelly; cats eyes; sea walnut comb jelly.
Description: Transparent, egg-shaped organism with 2 long tentacles.
Size: To ⁵/₈" (1.5 cm) in diameter; tentacles 6" (15 cm) long.
Habitat: Found near shore, often in large numbers.
Range: Alaska to Baja California.
Notes: This is the only common species of comb jelly likely to be found in Pacific Northwest waters. Comb jellies use sticky cells on the tentacles, rather than stinging cells, to capture food. They are often found in spring and summer swimming in large swarms. Occasionally they wash up on the beach. Each individual is both male and female. Eggs and sperm are released from the mouth to be fertilized in open water. This species has been called a voracious carnivore, as swarms can severely reduce schools of young fish. Most comb jellies are bioluminescent, but this species cannot produce its own light.

Phylum Cnidaria

Sea Anemones & Cup Corals • Class Anthozoa

Sea anemones, like their relatives the jellies, possess nematocysts (stinging cells), primarily on their tentacles. The animal uses its nematocysts to sting its prey when contacted. If a person's hand touches the tentacles they only feel sticky, since the skin on our hands is too thick to allow penetration, but a sting-ing sensation was definitely felt by an individual who licked the tentacles of one species, using his much more sensitive tongue. (This technique is, however, not recommended!) Most anemones feed upon fishes, crabs, sea urchins, shrimps and similar prey. Habitat varies from the high intertidal zone to as deep as 30,000' (9,000 m) for some species in the Philippines.

The class Anthozoa includes both sea anemones and cup corals, anemone-like organisms with hard, cup-shaped skeletons.

›ORANGE CUP CORAL

Balanophyllia elegans

Other names: Orange-red coral; solitary coral.
Description: Bright orange, cup-shaped organism with hard outer seat-like shape surrounded by many small tentacles. Resembles a small anemone; its hard seat helps in identifying it correctly as a hard coral.
Size: To ½" (1.2 cm) in diameter.
Habitat: On shady sides and under rocks or boulders, low intertidal zone to water 70' (21 m) deep.
Range: BC to Baja California.
Notes: Identification of this species is made easily since no other orange stony coral is found intertidally in the Pacific Northwest. Its vivid orange color comes from a fluorescent pigment. Feeding is accomplished with small, transparent-like tentacles and a mouth which opens to trap food. Although this species is small, its presence is always a welcome splash of color.

⟩ TEN-TENTACLED ANEMONE
Halcampa decemtentaculata

Other name: Ten-tentacled burrowing anemone.
Description: White, cream or brown. It has 10 tentacles, as its name suggests.
Size: Disc to 1/4" (6 mm) in diameter; total length to 3/4" (2 cm).
Habitat: Lower intertidal zone, often buried among the roots of eelgrass (see p. 183).
Range: Vancouver Island to California.
Notes: Due to its size, this burrowing anemone can easily go unnoticed. Its column is buried and can sometimes reach 3" (8 cm) when fully extended. Tentacles and column can become somewhat translucent when extended. Little is known about the biology of this species.

⟩ MOONGLOW ANEMONE
Anthopleura artemisia

Other names: Green burrowing anemone; buried sea anemone; beach sand anemone.
Description: Overall coloration varies from brown to gray or olive-green. Slender, tapering, bright pink, orange, green or blue **tentacles with distinctive white bands**. Column is usually covered with sand and bits of shell.
Size: To 2" (5 cm) in diameter, with only disc and tentacles protruding above the surface.
Habitat: In sand or gravel on sheltered cobblestone or rocky shorelines, mid- or low intertidal zone and into the subtidal, in both exposed and sheltered locations.
Range: Alaska to southern California.
Notes: The species gets its name from the luminous quality often exhibited by the tentacles. The moonglow anemone is usually found in sandy areas, where it is attached to a large shell or rock, buried up to 12" (30 cm) beneath the surface. The aggregating anemone (see below) can look similar when living in sand, but it lacks the white bands on its tentacles.

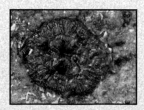

› Aggregating Anemone

Anthopleura elegantissima

Other names: Clustering aggregate anemone; pink-tipped green anemone; surf anemone.
Description: Coloration variable. The anemone displays **pale green tentacles with pinkish or purple tips** and a pale green to gray column.
Size: Isolated individuals may grow to 10" (25 cm) in diameter, 20" (51 cm) high. Aggregating individuals, however, reach less than a third of this size.
Habitat: In colonies attached to rocks above the low tide line and in tidepool situations on exposed and protected shores with active currents. The presence of sand seems to be important where this species colonizes.
Range: Alaska to Baja California.
Notes: Aggregating anemones are well known for their ability to multiply asexually by dividing into two identical individuals. As a result, they are capable of colonizing large rock surfaces as genetic clones. At some locations, their clones completely carpet entire rocks. Sexual reproduction is also possible.

By necessity, this species must be very tolerant of harsh conditions including exposure to the sun, wind and waves. They are often observed in a closed position, out of water, which prevents them from drying out. However, this changes their appearance dramatically.

This anemone's predators include the shaggy mouse nudibranch (see p. 84) and the leather star (see p. 131).

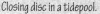
Closing disc in a tidepool.

› GIANT GREEN ANEMONE
Anthopleura xanthogrammica

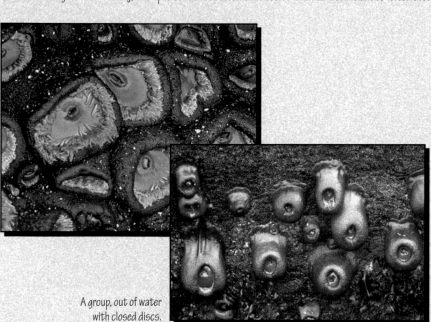

Other names: Green anemone; rough anemone; solitary anemone.

Description: Disc and tentacles are a beautiful emerald green, short column is olive-brown. Sand and shell fragments are commonly found in disc.

Size: To 12" (30 cm) in diameter, 12" (30 cm) high.

Habitat: On exposed rocky shores, intertidal to water deeper than 50' (15 m).

Range: Alaska to Panama.

Notes: This sea anemone is found in both a solitary existence and in groups, often in tidepools. Microscopic green algae live inside the tentacles, giving the animal its green color. This species attains adult size at age 14 or 15 months and has been known to live longer than 30 years in captivity.

The giant green anemone has been utilized by man in different ways. The Haida historically cooked it carefully over a fire before eating it. More recently, this species has been used as the source for a heart stimulant to vertebrates.

A group, out of water with closed discs.

❯ BROODING ANEMONE
Epiactis lisbethae

Description: Red, purple or green with **fine white pin-striping over entire animal, including middle portion of column.** As many as 300 small young are often found on the column, arranged in as many as 5 rows.
Size: To 2–3" (5–8 cm) in diameter, about 1½" (4 cm) high.
Habitat: On rocks in areas of rough water such as surge channels, low intertidal zone to subtidal waters. They often find sufficient shelter on undersides of boulders.
Range: Bamfield, BC to Coos Bay, Oregon.
Notes: For years this anemone was thought to be the same species as the similar proliferating anemone (below). Young anemones are typically found on the columns of both species, but the brooding anemone grows to be a larger species that can carry several hundred young at one time. White pinstriping is also found on its entire column.

Individuals are sometimes found without young.

The sexes are separate in this species with only females brooding their young.

❯ PROLIFERATING ANEMONE
Epiactis prolifera

Other names: Brooding anemone; small green anemone.
Description: Green, brown or red with **white pin-stripes on base, that do not extend to center of column.** Young of various sizes are usually present, up to 30 at one time crowded into a single row.
Size: Normally to 1¼" (3 cm) in diameter, 1" (2.5 cm) high.

Habitat: In unprotected sites with eel-grass, kelp beds and the sides of rocks providing habitat, high tide line to water 30' (9 m) deep.
Range: Alaska to La Jolla, California.
Notes: This anemone has a sex life similar to that of orchids, referred to as gynodioecy. Young adults are usually female. As mothers, they grow in size and they also grow testes. Upon full maturity they are hermaphrodites, having both testes and ovaries.

The eggs develop within the digestive cavity of the parent, exit through the mouth and eventually attach themselves to the middle of the parent's column. Later the young move away from the parent to venture forth on their own.

❯ RED-BEADED ANEMONE
Urticina coriacea

Other names: Beaded anemone; leathery anemone; stubby rose anemone; formerly *Tealia coriacea*.

Description: Short red and gray tentacles with white bands. Thick column varies in color from brownish-red to hot pink with thick sucker-like tubercles covered by sand and shell debris. As a result, column is normally hidden from view.

Size: To 4" (10 cm) in diameter, 5 1/2" (14 cm) high.

Habitat: Usually found half-buried in sand or gravel or situated in gravel-filled crevices, low intertidal zone to water 50' (15 m) deep.

Range: Alaska to central California.

Notes: This anemone attaches itself to rocks or other solid objects beneath the surface, leaving only its crown visible. It is commonly found in shallow, rocky intertidal areas. Its chief enemy is the leather star (see p. 131). Little else is known about this anemone's biology.

The disc of this red-beaded anemone is open,

while this disc is closing in a tidepool.

This individual has temporarily turned its stomach inside out.

›PAINTED ANEMONE
Urticina crassicornis

Other names: Red and green anemone; Christmas anemone;
northern red anemone; dahlia anemone; mottled anemone; formerly *Tealia crassicornis*.

Description: Column varies considerably from green with red
blotches to solid color range of light yellow-brown, white, green
or occasionally totally red, as commonly found in Puget Sound.
Small wart-like cells may or may not be present on column.
Color of tentacles generally similar to or somewhat lighter
than column. No debris attached to column of this species.

Size: Normally to 4" (10 cm) but can reach 10" (25 cm) in
diameter; to 10" (25 cm) high.

A typically colored individual.

Habitat: In protected sites such as under ledges or vertical
rock surfaces, between low intertidal and subtidal zones.

Range: Alaska to central California.

Notes: The painted anemone has been known to live to 80 years in captivity. Young
individuals are normally found higher intertidally, while occasionally the tidepooler
can view older, larger specimens at the lowest of tides. These large individuals have
also been described by some observers as "obscene" for the manner in which they
may hang from their substrate. This circumpolar species is referred to as the
thick-petaled rose anemone along the east coast.

A large white-spotted anemone hangs from a boulder.

›WHITE-SPOTTED ANEMONE
Urticina lofotensis

Other name: White-spotted rose anemone.

Description: Bright scarlet red column, small white spots
arranged in longitudinal rows.

Size: To 6" (15 cm) high, 4" (10 cm) in diameter.

Habitat: Low intertidal zone to water 50' (15 m) deep.

Range: BC to San Diego, California.

Notes: This species is truly beautiful to view, but unfortu-
nately, not much is known about its biology. It is sometimes
found hanging from the side of a rock or boulder and in some
cases hidden from view under seaweed. Smaller individuals
are normally found intertidally. This anemone is also a circumpolar species, found on the north Atlantic coast.

▷PLUMOSE ANEMONE
Metridium senile

Other names: The many common names for the giant plumose anemone (see next page) have been used for this species as well.

Description: Smooth white, yellow, orange or brown in color, with fewer than 100 tentacles.

Size: Normally to 2" (5 cm) high but can reach 4" (10 cm); **to 2" (5 cm) in diameter at base**.

Habitat: Common in protected waters attached to hard objects such as wharves, dock pilings and rocks.

Range: Alaska to California.

Notes: This anemone is easily found as it is commonly attached to floating docks and similar sites throughout its range. It feeds on copepods and various invertebrate larvae.

White form on a dock, underwater.

Unlike its relative the giant plumose anemone (see below), this anemone reproduces asexually. In fact, a new anemone can arise from tissue left behind when this anemone moves along to a new site. The new individual is a clone of the original. It is truly amazing that this species and the giant plumose anemone fooled biologists for many years into believing that only the one species existed.

Closed (left) and open (right) individuals underwater.

Above the water.

> GIANT PLUMOSE ANEMONE

Metridium giganteum

Other names: Sun anemone; frilled anemone; powder puff anemone; white-plumed anemone.

Description: Column ranges in color from white to brown or orange. A cluster of more than 200 white tentacles crown a long, smooth column.

Size: 4–39" (10–100 cm) high, **to 4" (10 cm) in diameter at base**.

Habitat: Normally attached to rock substrates, primarily in subtidal waters but occasionally in low intertidal zone.

Range: Alaska to California.

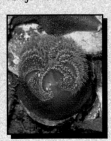

Notes: This large species is found on piers and pilings in areas of low salinity. At low tide it can sometimes be seen hanging from ledges assuming surreal-looking postures. Until a few years ago, this anemone was thought to be a form of the plumose anemone (see above). Biologists now know that the two forms are two separate species. The giant plumose anemone grows much larger, which is often the easiest method to identify it when it is contracted, out of water.

> STRIPED ANEMONE

Haliplanella luciae

Other name: Formerly *Haliplanella lineata*.

Description: Olive green overall, with pale orange or yellow stripes running up and down the column.

Size: To 3/4" (1.9 cm) high, 1/4" (6 mm) in diameter.

Habitat: On rocks and similar objects in shallow water, or salt marshes in high intertidal zone.

Range: Southern BC to southern California.

Notes: This anemone is thought to have been introduced accidentally in the late nineteenth century, when the Pacific oyster *Crassostrea gigas* was brought to North America for commercial purposes. Its small size makes it an easy species to overlook. The striped anemone, like other species, has specialized tentacles called catch tentacles which can be used in disputes with other anemones of the same or different species. These battles can be fatal to one or the other anemone.

A free-living scaleworm.

MARINE WORMS
Phyla Platyhelminthes, Nemertea, Annelida, Sipuncula

Marine worms are a collection of unrelated yet similar animal groups. These worms are classified in several phyla, including flatworms, ribbon worms, segmented worms and peanut worms.

FLATWORMS
Phylum Platyhelminthes

These unsegmented worms are characteristically flat and do not have blood or circulatory systems. Flatworms may have eyespots, which are not restricted to the head region. These organs merely detect the presence of light.

> LARGE LEAF WORM
Kaburakia excelsa

Other name: Leaf worm.
Description: Color varies from orange to brown. Tough, firm, oval body. 2 short retractable tentacles, each with an eyespot, near brain.
Size: To 4x2³/4" (10x7 cm), ¹/8" (3 mm) thick.
Habitat: Occasionally found around mussel beds or seaweeds and under rocks, sometimes in large numbers; intertidal zone.
Range: Sitka, Alaska to Newport Harbor, California.
Notes: This giant species responds negatively to sunlight. Approximately 50 minute light-sensitive eyespots are located along the margin. This worm glides over the substrate by using thousands of tiny cilia, blending in to its environment so well that it is often difficult to detect. There is a mouth on the lower or ventral side but no anus, thus wastes pass back through the worm's mouth to be expelled. It is believed that this species feeds on animals such as limpets.

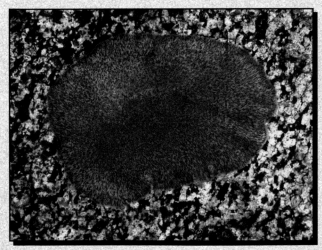

RIBBON WORMS
Phylum Nemertea

The worms in this group are more advanced than flatworms, with blood or circulatory systems. The ribbon worm has a retractable snout (proboscis) with either sticky glands or poisonous hooks to capture its prey.

❯ RED RIBBON WORM
Tubulanus polymorphus

Other names: Orange nemertean; orange ribbon worm; formerly *Carinella rubra*.

Description: Vivid red or orange. Elongated round, soft body with no distinct markings on the head.

Size: To 3' (90 cm) long, and to an amazing 10' (3 m) in large specimens, but often somewhat contracted due to its elastic nature. To $^3/_{16}$" (5 mm) wide.

Habitat: Among mussels, in gravel or under rocks in quiet areas, sometimes in higher numbers, rocky low intertidal zone to 164' (50 m) deep.

Range: Aleutian Islands, Alaska to San Luis Obispo County, California.

Notes: This highly visible worm can often be observed moving slowly along in intertidal pools, hunting for prey. Its slow movement and rounded shape are characteristic. Often common in spring and summer.

❯ TWO-SPOTTED RIBBON WORM
Amphiporus bimaculatus

Other names: Chevron amphiporus; thick amphiporus.

Description: Orange or brownish-red; short, stocky body. Lighter-colored **head has pair of dark triangular markings.**

Size: To 5" (12 cm) long.

Habitat: Usually in a rocky situation, low intertidal zone to water 450' (137 m) deep.

Range: Sitka, Alaska to Baja California.

Notes: This common species, which resembles a leech, can sometimes be seen swimming after it has been disturbed. It breeds in July in the southern portion of its range. Like many worms, this species shuns light. The 2 eye-like markings in the head region are not eyes; but tiny light-detecting organs located near these markings help the worm detect light and find its way to darkness.

SEGMENTED WORMS
Phylum Annelida

These worms are easily identified by the many visible rings that make up their bodies. Over 9,000 species of segmented worms have been identified. Many marine species are found on the sea bottom but are not restricted to it.

⟩ PROBOSCIS WORM
Glycera sp.

Other names: Beak thrower; bloodworm.
Description: Light-colored, iridescent body, long and earthworm-like. Elongated head resembles a tapered point, which can fire out a snout (proboscis) containing 4 hooks at the tip.
Size: To 14" (35 cm) long.
Habitat: In mud and muddy sand, in areas of eel-grass and protected sites under rocks, low intertidal zone to water 1,040' (315 m) deep.
Range: BC to Baja California.
Notes: 4 black jaws grace this worm's snout (proboscis), which it can evert rapidly to almost a third of its body length. The worm uses its proboscis to capture prey. It also extends the proboscis into the sand, where the end swells to act as an anchor in bringing the body forward. Please **exercise caution** if you handle this worm. Its remarkable proboscis can inflict quite a bite.

⟩ PILE WORM
Nereis vexillosa

Other names: Mussel worm; clamworm.
Description: Males iridescent blue-green, females dull green. Body is made up of approximately 200 segments, each of which has a pair of leg-like appendages. Species makes a strong first impression, thanks to pincer-like claws gracing snout (proboscis).
Size: To 12" (30 cm) long.
Habitat: Found in a wide variety of habitats, including sand and mud beaches, beneath rocks, on wharf pilings and in mussel beds, in **high to mid-intertidal zones** of protected shores to exposed shorelines. The pile worm builds a loose flexible tube from a mucous secretion binding sand and stones together.
Range: Alaska to San Diego, California.
Notes: The breeding season of this common species is linked to the full moons of summer. At this time, huge congregations can be observed at night using their flattened leg-like appendages for swimming. The males release their sperm, then the females release eggs. Once the breeding sequence is completed, both sexes perish. Please **exercise caution** when handling the pile worm. It has been known to deliver the occasional nasty bite! The giant pile worm (see below) is a similar species, but grows to 3' (90 cm) long.

> GIANT PILE WORM
Nereis brandti

Other name: Formerly *Neanthes brandti*.
Description: Snout (proboscis) bears large number of tooth-like projections. Posterior appendages have paddle-like lobes. Juveniles have about 160 segments, adults have about 230 segments.
Size: To an impressive 3.3' (1 m) long, occasionally to 5' (1.5 m) long.
Habitat: Buried deep in mud or sand, **very low intertidal zone** to subtidal waters.
Range: BC to southern California.
Notes: This worm is also known to swarm while spawning—a truly extraordinary sight for worms of this size! This behavior has been observed in spring and early summer in the southern part of the species' range. The giant pile worm is also found in the Siberian Pacific.

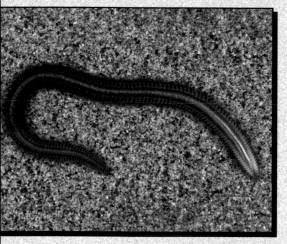

> SANDWORM
Nephtys sp.

Other name: Shimmy worm, sometimes misspelled *Nephthys*.
Description: Color varies. Body is beautifully iridescent. **No long tentacles in head region. Leg-like paddles (parapodia) look fuzzy** because of numerous hairs.
Size: To 12" (30 cm) long.
Habitat: Burrows in sand or sand-mud, mid-intertidal zone to subtidal waters 2,876' (869 m) deep.
Range: Alaska to Peru.
Notes: This rapid burrower everts a unique muscular proboscis to feed on worms and crustaceans. Like several other worms, it swims with a side-to-side wriggling movement aided by the paddling motions of its parapodia. A microscope is necessary to identify this species positively.

›EIGHTEEN-SCALED WORM
Halosydna brevisetosa

Other name: Armored scaleworm.
Description: Color ranges from gray, brown to reddish. Large powerful jaws; **18 pairs of overlapping scales.**
Size: To 4³/8" (11 cm) long.
Habitat: Low intertidal zone to water 1,800' (545 m) deep.
Range: Alaska to Baja California.
Notes: This worm can release one or more scales if it feels threatened, and generate a replacement in a mere 5 days. Like several other scaleworms, this one can live independently or commensally on a host. Those that choose a host often grow to twice the length of free-living individuals, perhaps because more food is available to the commensal worms.

Several other scaleworms are often seen intertidally, including the twelve-scaled worm *Lepidonotus squamatus*.

›FRAGILE SCALEWORM
Arctonoe fragilis

Other name: Frilled commensal scaleworm.
Description: Light in color, often matching color of host. 2 rows of ruffled and folded edges.
Size: To 3¹/2" (8.5 cm) long.
Habitat: Low intertidal zone to water 908' (275 m) deep.
Range: Alaska to San Francisco, California.
Notes: This worm feeds on detritus. It is often found on the underside of the mottled star (see p. 133), and several other species of sea stars also host it. Normally only one fragile scaleworm is found on a host at a time, but there have been reports of up to 4 at a time being found on a host.

>RED COMMENSAL SCALEWORM

Arctonoe pulchra

Other name: Scale worm.
Description: Brick red. Each scale may or may not display a single dark spot.
Size: To 2³/₄" (7 cm) long.
Habitat: In the cavity of several intertidal hosts (see Notes).
Range: Gulf of Alaska to Baja California.
Notes: This species, like several other scale-worms, feeds on detritus. It is found on the underside of a variety of organisms, including the rough keyhole limpet (see p. 62), giant Pacific chiton (p. 61), leather star (p. 131), California sea cucumber (p. 140) and striped sun star (p. 132).

>RED-BANDED COMMENSAL SCALEWORM

Arctonoe vittata

Other names: Scale worm; formerly *Polynoe vittata.*
Description: Pale yellow with a red-brown band; series of scales along the edges of the back.
Size: To 4" (10 cm) long.
Habitat: Low intertidal zone to water 800' (244 m) deep.
Range: Pacific coast.

Notes: Some individuals are free living, some live commensally. Hosts vary from the rough keyhole limpet (see p. 62) and giant Pacific chiton (p. 61) to 9 species of sea stars, including the leather star (p. 131) and Pacific blood star (p. 132). The host attracts the worm by releasing a chemical scent. This species actually helps protect its host from predators, such as the purple star (p. 135), by biting at the predator's tube feet when it attacks. It is definitely in this worm's best interest to ensure its host continues to live!

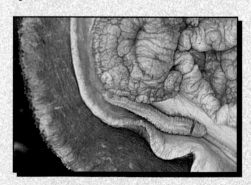

>Pacific Lugworm
Abarenicola pacifica

Other name: Lugworm.
Description: Light orange with branched gills along the body (color best viewed under water).
Size: To 6" (15 cm) long.
Habitat: On sand-mud beaches, high intertidal zone.
Range: Alaska to Humboldt Bay, California.
Notes: Telltale castings of mud and sand often indicate the presence of this species. Beneath the slender fecal casting lies a J-shaped burrow harboring the lugworm, which extracts bacteria and organic debris from the sand. When this worm is first uncovered, its long body is greenish in color, but once immersed in water, this seemingly unattractive creature contracts and quickly changes to a pleasant-looking worm with the hemoglobin of its body becoming visible. If left long enough, the gills eventually expand and become bright red. Lugworms have been used as bait by fishermen in Europe and elsewhere. Another species, the black lugworm *Abarenicola claparedi*, is a similar, dark-colored worm found much lower on seashores.

The distinctive sand casting.

>Bloodworm
Euzonus sp.

Other name: Formerly *Thoracophelia*.
Description: Bright red, because of hemoglobin in the blood.
Size: To 1¹/₂" (4 cm) long.
Habitat: On sand beaches, around mid-intertidal zone, burrowing to depth of 4–12" (10–30 cm) below the surface.
Range: Vancouver Island, BC to Baja California.
Notes: Bloodworms are often found in very high numbers, frequently in a band less than 3' (1 m) wide along the shore. They burrow deeper into the sand as the water slowly recedes and the sand dries out. These worms are very important food for a wide variety of migrating shorebirds.

Many tiny holes indicate the bloodworm's presence.

› SPAGHETTI WORM

Thelepus sp.

Other names: Shell binder worm; curly terebellid; hairy gilled worm.

Description: Pinkish body with long, white to flesh-colored tentacles on 3 pairs of branched, plumed red gills. Tentacles are coiled and extend many times the length of the worm.

Size: To 6" (15 cm) long.

Habitat: In crude tubes of sand and mud; under stones, cobble or boulders, near low tide mark.

Range: Pacific coast.

Notes: This distinctive worm lives inside a tube it constructs from sand and debris. Often the only visible sign of its presence is the waving of thin white gills and dark tentacles from beneath a rock. Like many other invertebrates that live beneath rocks, this worm is fragile. Rocks and boulders must be carefully returned to their original positions so that the worms' soft bodies are protected. If left exposed, they make easy prey for fish and other animals.

› BASKET-TOP TUBE WORM

Pista elongata

Other names: Fibre tube worm; elongate terebellid worm.

Description: Pinkish body enclosed in unique fibrous tube.

Size: To 8" (20 cm) long; tube to 3" (7.5 cm) long.

Habitat: In tubes, in crevices or under rocks, mid-intertidal zone to subtidal depths of 40' (12 m).

Range: BC to Panama.

Notes: This worm displays an ornate, fibrous, spongy basket-like structure at the end of its tube. Feeding is accomplished by extending the long tentacles to capture tiny food particles in the water, then moving the particles to the mouth of the tube with tiny cilia.

>NORTHERN FEATHER DUSTER WORM
Eudistylia vancouveri

Other names: Parchment tube worm; plume worm.
Description: Tough, horny tube encloses worm. Green and purple tentacles grace top of worm when expanded and submerged in water.
Size: To 10" (25 cm) long, ½" (1.2 cm) wide; head (tentacles) expands to 2" (5.1 cm) in diameter.
Habitat: Often found in large clusters, in crevices of rocky shores or on floats or pilings, low intertidal zone.
Range: Alaska to central California.
Notes: This species is sometimes found in areas of heavy surf. The parchment-like tube is so tough that it is difficult or impossible to remove it by hand from its supporting rock. If the tube breaks, the worm repairs it rather than building a new one. This worm's feathery tentacles, which draw both food and oxygen from the water, have light-sensitive eyespots which close with the slightest shadow.

One worm with its tentacles expanded.

• •

>CALCAREOUS TUBE WORM
Serpula vermicularis

Other names: Red tube worm; includes *Serpula columbiana*.
Description: White tube is graced with many branched tentacles arranged in 2 spirals. Color of tentacles ranges widely from red to orange, pink and other colors, all with white banding.
Size: To 2½" (6.5 cm) long.
Habitat: On rocks in tidepools and stones in sheltered and exposed sit-uations, low intertidal zone to water 330' (100 m) deep.

Range: Alaska to northern California.
Notes: In 1767 the calcareous tube worm was first named by Carolus Linnaeus, the creator of the system by which we still classify all plants and animals. This very common worm has a visible red trap door (operculum) when its tentacles are retracted in the tube. The frilly circular tentacles filter tiny microorganisms from the water but disappear instantly with the slightest disturbance.

• •

> SPIRAL TUBE WORM

Spirorbis sp. (and others)

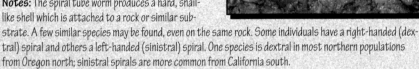

Other name: Tiny tube worm.
Description: Small white snail-like shell.
Size: To 1/4" (6 mm) in diameter.
Habitat: Attached to rocks, shells and various seaweeds, low intertidal zone to subtidal depths.
Range: Pacific coast.
Notes: The spiral tube worm produces a hard, snail-like shell which is attached to a rock or similar substrate. A few similar species may be found, even on the same rock. Some individuals have a right-handed (dextral) spiral and others a left-handed (sinistral) spiral. One species is dextral in most northern populations from Oregon north; sinistral spirals are more common from California south.

PEANUT WORMS
Phylum Sipuncula

The peanut worm has two parts, one of which is much larger and more globular than the other. Only 320 species in this small group have been identified worldwide.

> AGASSIZ'S PEANUT WORM

Phascolosoma agassizii

Other name: Peanut worm.
Description: Light to dark brown, occasionally with purple or dark brown spots. Narrow, extendable neck-like portion of body has dark bands, followed by a wider, rough body section.
Size: To 4 3/4" (12 cm) long, 1/2" (1.3 cm) wide; often much smaller.
Habitat: In sand under rocks or among the root-like holdfasts of seaweeds, above low intertidal zone.
Range: Alaska to Baja California.
Notes: This peanut worm is the most commonly encountered species living along the Pacific coast. A few short tentacles, located near the mouth, are used to feed on detritus when this worm leaves its resting spot. This species is also known to live in burrows abandoned by hole borers such as the rough piddock (see p. 100).

Empty shells of butter clam *Saxidomus gigantea* and Lewis's moonsnail *Polinices lewisii*.

MOLLUSKS AND BRACHIOPODS
Phyla Mollusca & Brachiopoda

The mollusks are a large group (phylum) of creatures, including the chitons, abalone, limpets, snails, nudibranchs, clams, mussels and octopus. Mollusks have inhabited salt water, fresh water, land and even the air for short distances. They are highly diverse, having only a few characteristics in common. All mollusks possess a fold of soft flesh (mantle) which encloses several glands, such as the stomach and the shell-producing glands. Many mollusks also have a toothed or rasping tongue (radula) and a shell covering. Scientists estimate there are some 50,000 to 130,000 species of mollusks in the world.

Chitons • Class Polyplacophora

Chitons, sometimes referred to as sea cradles and coat-of-mail shells, range in color from bright to well camouflaged. They have a series of 8 plates or valves held together by an outer girdle. Individuals in this group can be difficult to identify as they are very similar in appearance.

>LINED CHITON

Tonicella lineata

Other name: Lined red chiton.
Description: Striking colors varying from pink to orange-red. This chiton is named for the alternating light and dark zigzag lines on the plates. Outer girdle is dark, often with light blotches.
Size: To 2" (5 cm) long, often much shorter.
Habitat: On rocks with encrusting coralline algae, low intertidal to shallow subtidal zones.
Range: Alaska to Channel Islands, California.
Notes: This is one of the most beautiful chitons found in the Pacific Northwest, with brilliant colors that are not easily forgotten. Its color often closely matches the pink coralline algae on which it is most commonly found feeding. This chiton's main enemies are the purple star (see p. 135) and the six-rayed star (p. 133).

›WHITE-LINED CHITON
Tonicella insignis

Other names: Red chiton; formerly *Tonicella submarmorea*.
Description: Distinctive maroon red valves with white zigzag lines.
Size: To 2" (5 cm) long.
Habitat: Low intertidal zone to subtidal depths of 170' (52 m).
Range: Alaska to Oregon.
Notes: The northern clingfish (see p. 149) has been found to feed on this chiton in some areas.

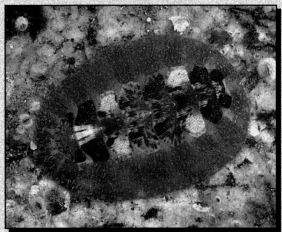

HAIRY CHITON
Mopalia ciliata

Description: Valves vary in color and are often very colorful. Wide outer girdle, covered in **soft hairs**, with a distinct notch at the rear.
Size: To 3" (7.5 cm) long.
Habitat: On protected sites, such as under rocks, mid- to low intertidal zones.
Range: Alaska to Baja California.
Notes: This chiton feeds at night and on cloudy days, grazing on tiny animals and diatoms which it finds attached to rock. Its rasping tongue (radula) contains magnetite, a hard oxide of iron which aids the animal greatly while feeding. A similar species, the mossy chiton (see below), can be distinguished by the stiff hairs on its girdle. A gentle touch will determine its texture.

⟩ MOSSY CHITON
Mopalia muscosa

Description: Valves or dorsal plates are brown, gray or black, occasionally with white stripes. Girdle is covered in **stiff hairs**, making it look somewhat fuzzy. Notch present at rear.
Size: To 2³/4" (7 cm) long.
Habitat: Often on top of rocks and in tidepools, intertidal zone.
Range: Alaska to Baja California.
Notes: This species is often observed in daylight since it does not hide under rocks as most chitons do. Instead, it stays in one place until darkness falls, when it begins feeding on algae. This species can be distinguished from the hairy chiton (above) by gently touching its girdle, which has stiff hairs. Individuals have been found to have a home range of 20" (50 cm) in a tidepool which forms their permanent home. The mossy chiton is often found with a variety of other intertidal life forms growing on its back. Accumulations of silt do not affect it.

⟩ WOODY CHITON
Mopalia lignosa

Description: Valves can vary widely in color from brown, blue, green to gray, often with additional stripes in brown. **Stiff hairs stem from light-colored spots on girdle.**
Size: To 2³/4" (7 cm) long.
Habitat: Intertidal and subtidal zones.
Range: Alaska to California.
Notes: This common species is often found under or on the sides of large rocks. It feeds on a variety of food, including diatoms and more than two dozen species of other algae, chiefly sea lettuce (*Ulva* sp.). The woody chiton has been observed reproducing in captivity. Females release their eggs in single file, and the eggs bunch up behind them. Males release their sperm into the water in spurts, fertilizing the eggs.

>Swan's Mopalia
Mopalia swanii

Description: Valves are highly variable in color, ranging from yellow, orange, red, green to brown. Wide girdle, mottled with various shades of brown and soft and velvety to the touch. Prominent cleft at posterior end of girdle.
Size: To 2¹/₂" (6 cm) long.
Habitat: On undersides of rocks and under ledges, intertidal zone.
Range: Unalaska Island, Alaska to Malibu, California.
Notes: This mopalia has been observed feeding as it moves along its substrate, cleaning everything off as it goes and apparently having few food preferences. Its valves can include patterns, speckles and stripes, and combinations of these.

>Red-flecked Mopalia
Mopalia spectabilis

Description: Olive-colored valves with red or orange zigzag markings, often with brown and blue-green sections included. Wide, hairy girdle with cleft at posterior.
Size: To 2³/₄" (7 cm) long.
Habitat: Under ledges and on bottoms of rocks, intertidal zone to water 33' (10 m) deep.
Range: Kodiak Island, Alaska to Baja California.
Notes: The red-flecked mopalia feeds on a variety of invertebrates, including sponges, hydroids, bryozoans and sea squirts. A species of scaleworm is sometimes found in the mantle cavity. This species often carries hitchhikers attached to its plates, including encrusting bryozoans and the shells of small tube worms.

› COOPER'S CHITON
Lepidozona cooperi

Other name: Formerly *Ischnochiton cooperi*.
Description: Color ranges from dull gray to olive or brown. Plates have raised portions on the sides.
Size: To 1¹/₂" (4 cm) long.
Habitat: Under rocks, in intertidal zone to water 65' (20 m) deep on the open coast.
Range: Neah Bay, Washington to Baja California.
Notes: This chiton, like most of its relatives, is usually found under rocks away from sunlight, which ensures that it will not be easily seen by predators and will not dry out in the heat of the sun.

› MERTEN'S CHITON
Lepidozona mertensii

Description: Valves range from brown to brick-red or purple in color, with intermittent white lines, giving this species a mottled look. Tiny knob-like projections give it a sandpapery appearance.
Size: To 2" (5 cm) long.
Habitat: Under rocks, in low intertidal zone to water 300' (90 m) deep.
Range: Alaska to California.

Notes: This is a common species, especially in the northern part of its range. Its colors help to identify it. Light-sensitive organs called aesthetes are found on the plates of this species, as in all chitons. These specialized organs help chitons retreat from light, since they do not have eyes.

> THREE-RIB CHITON
Lepidozona trifida

Other name: Formerly *Ischnochiton (Tripoplax) trifidus.*
Description: Typically reddish-brown to orange valves. 2 radiating lines separate middle plates into 3 sections. All members of this genus have several slits on each side of the middle (intermediate) plates.
Size: To 2½" (6 cm) long.
Habitat: On rocks, in intertidal zone to water 365' (110 m) deep.
Range: Alaska to Puget Sound, Washington.
Notes: A hand lens is a handy tool for looking at the minute granules covering the shells or valves of this species. Like most chitons, this one feeds on algae.

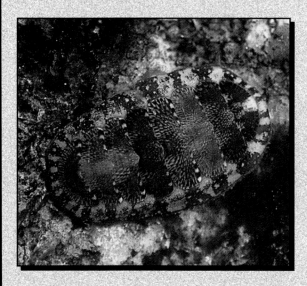

> GOULD'S BABY CHITON
Lepidochiton dentiens

Other name: Formerly *Cyanoplax dentiens.*
Description: Somewhat elongated shape, dark girdle with light mottling or white spots. Color of plates varies greatly, often dark brown or green.
Size: To ½" (1.3 cm) long.
Habitat: Low to mid-intertidal zone, occasionally higher in tidepools.
Range: Alaska to California.
Notes: True to its common name, this is truly a small species—much smaller than most other chitons found intertidally.

⟩PAINTED DENDROCHITON

Dendrochiton flectens

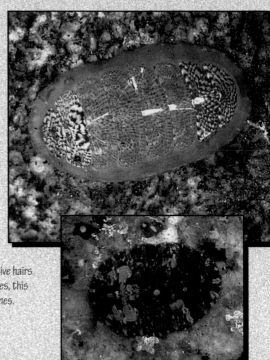

Other names: Formerly *Basiliochiton flectens*; *Basiliochiton heathii*; *Trachydermon heathii*; *Lepidochitona heathii*.

Description: Quite variable in color, often with a bright orange girdle. Smooth surface overall. Single long hairs along the girdle, especially at posterior end. These hairs may be branched.

Size: To 1¹/₈" (3 cm) long.

Habitat: In rocky areas, from very low intertidal zone to water 80' (24 m) deep.

Range: Sitka, Alaska to San Pedro, California.

Notes: This is an uncommon intertidal chiton, easy to identify in the field because of the distinctive hairs found on the girdle. Like several other marine species, this chiton has a long history of different scientific names.

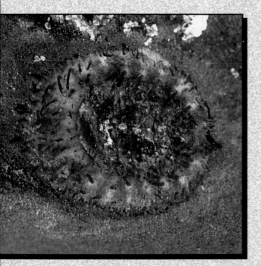

⟩VEILED-CHITON

Placiphorella velata

Other names: Veiled Pacific chiton; hooded chiton.

Description: Pink, blue and olive valves. Girdle is often red and noticeably wider near the head.

Size: To 2¹/₂" (6 cm) long.

Habitat: On rocks and under ledges, in more exposed areas of the low intertidal zone to water 65' (20 m) deep.

Range: Alaska to Baja California.

Notes: The veiled-chiton is able to capture its prey in a remarkable way—by using the front portion of its girdle as a flap to seize its food. Small crustaceans and worms amble beneath this upraised hood, which is quickly lowered to trap the prey. Like other chitons, this one also grazes on foods such as encrusting algae.

›Black Katy Chiton
Katharina tunicata

Other names: Leather chiton; black chiton.
Description: A brown to black girdle covers most of this chiton. A white diamond shape is left uncovered on the top of each valve.
Size: To 4³/4" (12.1 cm) long.
Habitat: Commonly associated with exposed, rocky shorelines, mid-intertidal zone.
Range: Alaska to California.
Notes: This species is often found exposed during the day, feeding on algae growing on wave-washed rocks. It is large enough to have been used as food by coastal aboriginal people at one time. This chiton has a life span of only 3 years.

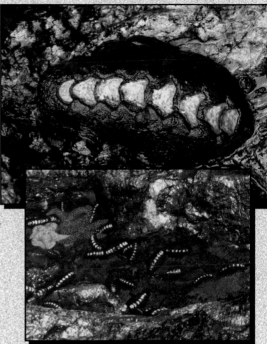

›Giant Pacific Chiton
Cryptochiton stelleri

Other names: Gumboot chiton; giant chiton; giant red chiton.
Description: Red-brown girdle completely covers plates on dorsal side.
Size: To 13" (33 cm) long.
Habitat: Low intertidal zone to subtidal water 65' (20 m) deep.
Range: Alaska to California.
Notes: This species is often called the gumboot chiton, probably because of its rubbery appearance. It feeds on red algae and is known to live longer than 20 years. Small individuals were once considered edible by coastal aboriginal people. The giant Pacific chiton hosts a worm (red-banded commensal scaleworm, see p. 48) that can live in the grooves on the underside of the chiton's body. The lurid rocksnail *Ocinebrina lurida*, which grows only to 1¹/2" (4 cm) long, has been known to attack this chiton, acclaimed as the largest chiton in the world. But the snail merely eats a shallow pit in the chiton's back.

Gastropods (Abalone, Limpets, Snails) • Class Gastropoda

The gastropods are a diverse group of invertebrates with few features in common, besides the muscular "foot" running along the underside of the body for locomotion (gastropod means "stomach foot"). Grazers, herbivores, scavengers and predators of many kinds all have a specialized tooth-bearing tongue (radula) for feeding. Another specialized organ—the otocyst, similar to our hearing apparatus—can also be found in the foot of many mollusks, but is used to maintain balance.

⟩NORTHERN ABALONE
Haliotis kamtschatkana

Other name: Pinto abalone.
Description: Shell has reddish or mottled exterior and beautiful mother-of-pearl interior. 4–6 respiration holes on dorsal side of shell.
Size: To 6" (15 cm) long.
Habitat: Low intertidal zone to water 50' (15 m) deep.
Range: Aleutian Islands, Alaska to San Pedro, California.
Notes: This abalone is thought to live to 50 years. A wide variety of marine life can often be found growing on the shell of this species. Its predators include the sea otter, red rock crab (see p. 120), cabezon, octopus and man. In the past, coastal aboriginal people ate abalone, and used the shells to make ornaments and fish hooks. In the last century or so, people have harvested this and other abalone species to the extent that populations are extremely reduced. Northern abalone are now protected from harvesting in the hope that their numbers will increase.

⟩ROUGH KEYHOLE LIMPET
Diodora aspera

Description: Color varies from light brown to gray, often with color banding. Prominent off-center opening at apex of shell. Ridges radiate from top and concentric lines cross the ridges at right angles.
Size: To 2³/₄" (7 cm) long.
Habitat: On rocky beaches, low intertidal to subtidal zones.
Range: Alaska to southern California.
Notes: The rough keyhole limpet has a large number of teeth on its tongue (radula) for grazing on seaweed attached to rock. To protect itself from predators such as the purple star (see p. 135), this limpet erects a thin, soft mantle to cover its shell and prevent the star from attaching with its tube feet. The red-banded commensal scaleworm (p. 48) is sometimes found on the underside of this limpet.

›HOODED PUNCTURELLA
Cranopsis cucullata

Other names: Helmet puncturella; *Puncturella cucullata.*
Description: White shell, with many raised ribs radiating from apex, and elongated slit behind top. The top can be noticeably hooked at the tip.
Size: To 1½" (4 cm) long.
Habitat: On rocks, low intertidal zone to water 660' (200 m) deep; more common subtidally.
Range: Alaska to Baja California.
Notes: The shell is oval in shape, nearly as high as it is long. The elongated slit in the shell reveals it to be one of the keyhole limpets.

›WHITECAP LIMPET
Acmaea mitra

Other names: Dunce-cap limpet; Chinamen's hat limpet.
Description: Shell is white or pink (see below) and somewhat cone-shaped. Shell interior bears horseshoe-shaped muscle scar.
Size: To 1" (2.5 cm) high.
Habitat: On rocky beaches, low intertidal to shallow subtidal zones.
Range: Alaska to California.
Notes: This limpet is often found covered in pink encrusting coralline algae (see p. 170), which also happens to be its prime food. The limpet's foot is strong enough to keep it from being washed away in the strongest of waves along the exposed coast.

>SHIELD LIMPET
Lottia pelta

Other name: *Collisella pelta.*
Description: Brown oval shell exterior with a variety of markings, occasionally with wavy edge. **Apex of shell is relatively high.**
Size: To 2⅛" (5.4 cm) long and ⅝" (1.5 cm) high.

Habitat: On rocks and among mussel beds, between high and low intertidal zones. Also found on various species of brown algae, including the surf-loving sea palm (see p. 165).
Range: Alaska to Mexico.
Notes: The limpet, like many other mollusks, enlarges its own shell. A group of glands around the edge of the mantle secrete a "liquid shell," made primarily of carbonate of lime, which hardens over time. In this way, the limpet's home is always the correct size. This limpet is similar to another species, the plate limpet (see below), which possesses a very flat shell.

A shield limpet rests on the stipe of this sea palm.

>PLATE LIMPET
Tectura scutum

Other name: *Notoacmaea scutum.*
Description: Often gray to greenish in color with off-white rectangular blotches radiating from top of the flat, oval shell. **Apex of shell is relatively low.**
Size: To 2" (5.1 cm) long.
Habitat: On rocks, high to low intertidal zones.

Range: Alaska to Baja California.
Notes: The plate limpet can be distinguished from other species by its brown tentacles, but these can be seen only if the limpet is active and not pressed tight against the substrate. This limpet tries to escape when various predatory sea stars are detected. Green algae are occasionally seen growing on its shell.

>RIBBED LIMPET
Lottia digitalis

Other names: Finger limpet; fingered limpet; *Collisella digitalis.*
Description: Overall color is gray with green-ish-brown bands. Shell is elliptical (one end narrower than the other), several prominent ribs radiate from top. Edge of shell is somewhat wavy.
Size: To 1" (2.5 cm) long.
Habitat: In rocky areas, splash zone to high intertidal zone, often in the shade.
Range: Alaska to Mexico.
Notes: One study showed that the greatest distance a ribbed limpet wandered from its established territory was only 3' (90 cm). The shape of the shell's outer edge matches precise-

ly the rock area which is its home. This close fit is very helpful in preventing a predator from removing the limpet from its substrate.

• •

>FILE LIMPET
Lottia limatula

Other name: Formerly *Collisella limatula.*
Description: Shell is relatively flat. Fine, toothed ribs radiate from the off-center apex.
Size: To 1³/₄" (4.5 cm) long.
Habitat: Mid- to lower intertidal zones.
Range: Southern BC to Baja California.
Notes: This is an uncommon species in the northern portion of its range. In the past, the file limpet has been observed from Newport, Oregon to Baja California. I have found individuals as far north as southern BC. Most limpets are vegetar-ians and as such have no proboscis, which flesh-eating (carnivorous) mollusks do. Individuals are found as separate sexes and their young start out life as free-swimming organisms. Occasionally albino specimens of this limpet are found. They have tan to cream-brown shell exteriors.

• •

❯ MASK LIMPET
Tectura persona

Other names: Speckled limpet; masked limpet; *Notoacmaea persona.*

Description: Color varies from blue-gray to brownish, with whitish rays stemming from top or a pattern of light gray spots. Several tiny white spots are found on top of shell. Apex is markedly off-center with a **slight hook-like shape near the tip**.

Size: To 1¹/₂" (4 cm) long.

Habitat: Prefers the dark of rock crevices or similar areas in high intertidal zone but comes out at night to feed.

Range: Alaska to central California.

Notes: Once the sun has set and darkness prevails, this limpet is busy feeding on algae. It has been calculated that a limpet of 1 square inch (6.5 cm²) requires a browsing area of encrusting seaweed covering 75 square inches (487 cm²) each year to survive.

❯ UNSTABLE LIMPET
Lottia instabilis

Other names: *Collisella instabilis, Acmaea instabilis.*

Description: Dark brown, occasionally with yellow-brown top. Edge of shell is saddle-shaped.

Size: To 1¹/₂" (3.5 cm) long.

Habitat: On holdfasts and stems (stipes) of various species of kelp, intertidal zone to subtidal depths of 240' (73 m).

Range: Kodiak Island, Alaska to San Diego, California.

Notes: This limpet's distinctive shape enables it to move easily on the stipes of seaweeds. If the shell is placed on a flat surface, it can rock back and forth. The unstable limpet feeds on various seaweeds, especially the split kelp (see p. 162).

⟩RED TURBAN
Astraea gibberosa

Other name: Formerly *Astraea inaequalis*.
Description: A thin brown paper-like covering (periostracum) covers the bright red to reddish-brown shell. Cone shape bears many ridges along each whorl.
Size: To 3" (7.5 cm) in diameter.
Habitat: On rocky shores, intertidal zone to subtidal water 200' (61 m) deep.
Range: Queen Charlotte Islands, BC to Baja California.
Notes: The shells and operculum of the red turban were valued highly by the Native peoples of BC, who may have traded them with Alaskan groups. This snail is edible.

⟩BLACK TURBAN
Tegula funebralis

Other name: Black top-shell.
Description: Purple-black shell with 4 rounded whorls.
Size: To 1¼" (3 cm) in diameter.
Habitat: On rocky shores, high to mid-intertidal zones.
Range: BC to lower California.
Notes: The turban eats only soft seaweed, using a specialized tongue (radula). Black turbans are believed to live as long as 100 years. Perhaps this is one reason why the tops of their shells are almost always worn to the underlying white shell layer. Black turbans were cracked open and eaten raw by the Native people of Vancouver Island, BC.

> PUPPET MARGARITE
Margarites pupillus

Other name: Little margarite.
Description: Variable color, including pink to orange. Aperture is a brilliant iridescent. Spiral ribbing is present on the somewhat flattened shell.
Size: To $3/4$" (1.7 cm) high.
Habitat: On sheltered sand and mud beaches, low intertidal to subtidal water 330' (100 m) deep.
Range: Alaska to San Diego, California.
Notes: The puppet margarite is especially common in the northern part of its range. Its predators include the dire whelk (see p. 75)

and frosted nudibranch (p. 83), which crushes the shell in its jaws. *Margarites* means "pearl," most likely referring to the interior color of the shell.

> PURPLE-RING TOPSNAIL
Calliostoma annulatum

Other names: Ringed top shell; purple-ringed topsnail.
Description: Pale yellow with bright purple bands. Cone-shaped shell, with several flattened whorls with beaded cords, protects the bright orange animal inside.
Size: To $1^{1}/2$" (4 cm) in diameter.
Habitat: On rocks, kelp and eel-grass (p. 183), low intertidal zone to subtidal water 100' (30 m) deep.
Range: Southern Alaska to northern Baja California.
Notes: This snail is usually associated with kelp, on which it feeds. It also eats hydroids, encrusting byzoans and detritus. In the northern portion of its range, this species is occasionally found intertidally, but this is not the case farther south. It is often observed by divers in subtidal waters.

>BLUE TOPSNAIL
Calliostoma ligatum

Other names: Blue top shell; ribbed topsnail; formerly *Calliostoma costatum.*
Description: Beautiful shell with brown striped exterior, nearly cone-shaped with several somewhat rounded whorls. Worn shells reveal underlying blue color.
Size: To 1" (2.5 cm) in diameter.
Habitat: On exposed, rocky beaches, low intertidal zone to subtidal water 100' (30 m) deep.
Range: Alaska to San Pedro, California.
Notes: This snail feeds on diatoms, kelp, detritus, hydroids and bryozoans. Its enemies include the six-rayed star (see p. 133) and the purple star (p. 135), and it has been found in the stomachs of lingcod. If the presence of a predatory sea star is detected, the speed of the blue topsnail doubles to $^{3/32}$" (2.9 mm) per second.

>SITKA PERIWINKLE
Littorina sitkana

Other name: Sitka littorine.
Description: Gray, brown or black shell, occasionally with bands of white, yellow or orange. Shell is **rounded overall, often with several raised ridges** on exterior.
Size: To $^{7/8}$" (2.4 cm) high.
Habitat: In eel-grass, seaweed or rocky shores, throughout intertidal zones, often in high intertidal zone on rockweed or other seaweeds.
Range: Alaska to Puget Sound, Washington.
Notes: This very common periwinkle can survive out of water about 50 percent of the time; in fact, it will actually suffocate if submerged under water for too long. A similar species, the checkered periwinkle (below), has a smooth, more elongated shell which lacks the ribbed channels.

❯ CHECKERED PERIWINKLE
Littorina scutulata

Other name: Checkered littorine.
Description: Smooth, brown or black elongated shell, often with white checkered spots.
Size: To 5/8" (1.6 cm) high.
Habitat: On various types of seaweed or rocky shores, high and middle intertidal zones.
Range: Alaska to California.
Notes: The largest checkered periwinkles are often found much higher up on shore than smaller individuals. Their enemies include several carnivorous gastropods and the six-rayed star (see p. 133). This family of snails have a unique foot, which is divided into two separate parts that move alternately. Some scientists believe land snails may have evolved from periwinkles.

❯ WIDE LACUNA
Lacuna vincta

Other names: Chink shell; wide chink-shell; common northern chink-shell; northern lacuna; Lacuna carinata.
Description: Variable colors, often dark brown with narrow bands of color. Shell features a wide aperture which flares outward. An additional small cavity or chink is located next to aperture.
Size: To 5/8" (1.6 cm) high.
Habitat: On algae of rocky shores, intertidal zone.
Range: Alaska to northern California.
Notes: This species is occasionally found in abundance. Females lay their eggs in jelly-like masses on the blades of seaweeds.

> MUDFLAT SNAIL

Batillaria cumingi

Other names: Screw shell; *Batillaria zonalis; Batillaria attramentaria.*
Description: Gray with brown bead-like finish; elongated, tapered shell with 8 or 9 whorls.
Size: To 1¼" (3.2 cm) high.
Habitat: On mud shorelines, high to mid-intertidal zones.
Range: BC to California.
Notes: This species was accidentally introduced with oysters from Japan. Its common name is an excellent choice since it is frequently found on mud flats. This snail has been found to reach incredible densities—7,000 individuals per square meter in ideal habitats. The mudflat snail's life span is estimated to be as long as 10 years.

> HOOKED SLIPPERSNAIL

Crepidula adunca

Description: Dark brown shell beneath a yellow skin-like periostracum. A beak-like hook at the tip overhangs posterior edge of shell.
Size: To 1" (2.5 cm) high.
Habitat: On rocks or on shells of other snails, intertidal zone.
Range: Queen Charlotte Islands, BC to southern California.
Notes: The hooked slippersnail is found riding the shells of various snails, including the black turban (see p. 67), which also may be used by hermit crabs. Slippersnails have both male and female parts but only become one sex at a time. Large slippersnails are females waiting for smaller male suitors. They prepare several small egg capsules, placing approximately 250 eggs in each. The capsules are attached to the surface on which the female resides and are guarded for approximately one month until the eggs hatch. The smaller slippersnails are males, which will become females and lay eggs as they grow older.

❯ OREGON TRITON
Fusitriton oregonensis

Other names: Hairy Oregon triton; *Argobuccinium oregonense*.
Description: Distinctive dark brown bristles cover the outer yellowish, skin-like periostracum. Sometimes the bristles are worn away, giving this species a "bald" appearance. Shell is made of 6 or 7 rounded whorls.
Size: To $4^{3/4}$" (12 cm) high.
Habitat: Low intertidal zone to water 300' (90 m) deep.
Range: Bering Sea to San Diego, California.
Notes: This carnivorous snail grows to be one of the largest found in the Pacific Northwest. Only small individuals are commonly found in the intertidal zone. Their distinctive eggs are laid in a circular cluster, sometimes referred to as sea corn. The first ones to hatch sometimes feed on neighboring eggs within the same group. This snail has been reported to feed occasionally on sea stars and sea urchins.

❯ LEWIS'S MOONSNAIL
Polinices lewisii

Other name: *Lunatia lewisi*.
Description: Yellowish shell with brown paper-like covering (periostracum). Shell is made of about 6 rounded whorls. Enormous pink, fleshy foot.
Size: To $5^{1/2}$" (14 cm) high.
Habitat: In sand, gravel or mud, low intertidal zone to subtidal water 165' (50 m) deep.
Range: Queen Charlotte Islands, BC to southern California.
Notes: This active carnivore plows through the sand, preying upon clams and other bivalves by drilling a hole in the shell of the prey. To protect itself, the foot contracts by ejecting water from perforations around the edge. This enables the animal to retreat inside, filling most of the shell. This species is also known for its distinctive large egg case, or "sand collar." Females crawl higher up on muddy sand beaches in the spring and summer to lay their eggs. The collar is formed around the extended mantle or fleshy foot and is made of two layers of sand sandwiching a layer of eggs, all held together with a mucous secretion. The moonsnail moves from beneath the collar once she is finished. She then leaves the egg case on the sand for the eggs to hatch.

The egg case has a distinctive shape.

The moonsnail drills through clam shells to feed on its prey.

>BOREAL WENTLETRAP
Opalia borealis

Other names: Chace's wentletrap;
Opalia wroblewskii; O. chacei.
Description: White, elongated shell
with several whorls, each with many
distinctive ribs.
Size: To 1" (2.5 cm) high.
Habitat: Intertidal to subtidal zones.
Range: Alaska to Puget Sound,
Washington.
Notes: The name *wentletrap* comes,

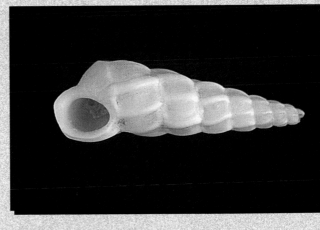

appropriately, from a Danish word meaning "spiral staircase." The snails in this group are known for their feeding habits. They are known to feed on various sea anemones, including the aggregating anemone (see p. 35) and
the giant green anemone (p. 36). The boreal wentletrap is one of several similar species of wentletraps found in
the Pacific Northwest.

>LEAFY HORNMOUTH
Ceratostoma foliatum

Other name: *Purpura foliata.*
Description: Color varies from gray to yellow or brown with 3 frills extending the
length of the shell. Species is noted for having a very strong shell with pronounced spiral
ribs.
Size: To 3¹/2" (8.9 cm) high.
Habitat: On rocky beaches, intertidal zone
to subtidal water 200' (60 m) deep.
Range: Sitka, Alaska to San Diego,
California.
Notes: This carnivore feeds on mussels and
barnacles by drilling holes through their
shells. Aggregations can often be found in late February and March when they gather to lay their yellow
eggs—occasionally on the shells of their buddies.

› FRILLED DOGWINKLE
Nucella lamellosa

Other names: Frilled whelk; wrinkled purple; wrinkled whelk; purple whelk; *Thais lamellosa*.

Description: Color ranges from white through yellow, orange, brown and purple. Heavy shell can be smooth in exposed situations while several frills are often present in sheltered areas.

Size: To 3¹/8" (8 cm) high.

Habitat: On exposed and sheltered rocky beaches, intertidal to subtidal zones.

Range: Bering Strait to California.

Notes: Large congregations of frilled dogwinkles are often found at the low tide mark in winter. At this time they breed, laying hundreds of yellow spindle-shaped eggs attached to the sides and undersides of rocks. These eggs are sometimes referred to as "sea oats." Each female is capable of laying up to 1,000 eggs per year, but maturity is reached at 4 years. Predators of this dogwinkle include the red rock crab (see p. 120), mottled star (p. 133) and purple star (p. 135).

› CHANNELLED DOGWINKLE
Nucella canaliculata

Other names: Channeled purple; *Thais canaliculata*.

Description: Color ranges from gray to yellowish. Several **grooved channels cover entire shell**.

Size: To 1¹/2" (4 cm) high.

Habitat: On rocky beaches, throughout intertidal zone.

Range: Aleutian Islands, Alaska to California.

Notes: The channelled dogwinkle feeds on mussels and barnacles and is often found moving among them. It drills a hole in the shell of its prey, then feeds on the delicacy inside. It has been found to require 1–2 days to complete the process of preparing (drilling) and feeding on one animal.

STRIPED DOGWINKLE
Nucella emarginata

Other names: Short-spired purple; rock-dwelling thais; rock whelk; emarginate dogwinkle; formerly *Thais emarginata*.
Description: Color varies from gray through yellow, brown or black, often with white bands on the ribs. **Bands on shell alternate between wide and narrow.**
Size: To 1" (2.5 cm) high.
Habitat: On rocky beaches, high and mid-intertidal zones.
Range: Bering Sea to Mexico.
Notes: This is quite a variable species. Two forms of it exist: an elongated form, often found in the more northerly sites, and a rounded form, to be seen in southern locations. The striped dogwinkle is a predator which drills holes in the shells of mussels, barnacles, limpets and other snails to feed on them. The sexes of this species are separate, but both have a penis. Their yellow spindle-shaped eggs are laid in the intertidal zone.

DIRE WHELK
Lirabuccinum dirum

Other names: Spindle shell; *Searlesia dira*.
Description: Brownish-gray with several low-rounded ribs on upper whorls.
Size: To 2" (5 cm) high.
Habitat: On exposed rocky beaches, intertidal zone to deep subtidal waters.
Range: Alaska to central California.
Notes: The dire whelk is more common in northern waters than in the south. This species is an active scavenger and carnivore, preying upon barnacles, mollusks and various worms. To feed, rather than drilling holes through the prey's shells as other snails do, it uses its proboscis to probe between and around their shells. Hermit crabs often use the empty shells of this species. The dire whelk is thought to live to 15 years.

A dire whelk rights itself.

ᐅ WRINKLED AMPHISSA
Amphissa columbiana

Other name: Wrinkled dove snail.
Description: Color varies from pink to mauve or yellow, often mottled with brown. Shell is made of several rounded body whorls with 20–24 longitudinal ribs on the second-last whorl.
Size: To 1⅛" (3 cm) high.
Habitat: On rocky beaches and mud, intertidal zone to water 96' (29 m) deep.
Range: Alaska to California.
Notes: This species gets its name from the ribs on the exterior of its shell. Its siphon or feeding tube is often seen extended while it searches for its next meal of carrion. This scavenger has also been found to be attracted to the food remains left by giant Pacific octopus (see p. 102) at its den.

ᐅ GIANT WESTERN NASSA
Nassarius fossatus

Other names: Channelled dog whelk; channelled basket snail.
Description: Exterior color ranges from gray to orange-brown, interior edge is a distinctive orange. A total of 7 whorls have many fine longitudinal ridges.
Size: To 2" (5 cm).
Habitat: In sheltered areas under rocks or buried in sand and mud, intertidal zone to water 60' (18 m) deep.
Range: Queen Charlotte Islands, BC to southern California.
Notes: This carnivore drills holes in clam and snail shells to feed on the inner tissues using its long proboscis or feeding organ. Its distinctive shell can sometimes be found lying on the beach.

❯Purple Olive
Olivella biplicata

Other name: Purple dwarf olive.
Description: Color varies from **near-white to lavender and dark purple**. Shell is smooth and shiny, indicating a large fleshy foot is present.
Size: To 1¼" (3 cm) high.
Habitat: On exposed sandy beaches, low intertidal zone to water 150' (46 m) deep.
Range: Sitka, Alaska to Baja California.
Notes: Distinctive tracks are left when this species burrows just under the surface of the sand, at the water's edge. This is one of few snails that has been observed swimming in order to escape predators. To accomplish this task, the remarkable purple olive engages in a wing-like rhythmic flapping of the folds in the outer fleshy body. By flapping the folds, the snail can swim upside down. The smooth shells of the Purple olive were admired and used as money and ornaments by Northwest Coast Native peoples. Strings of these shells have been found in their graves.

The purple olive moves under the sand, leaving a distinctive trail.

❯Baetic Olive
Olivella baetica

Other name: Little olive.
Description: Creamy with reddish-brown markings, often with purple or brown bands around each whorl. Shell is an elongated oval shape.
Size: To ¾" (1.9 cm) high.
Habitat: On exposed and sheltered sandy beaches, low intertidal zone to water 204' (62 m) deep.
Range: Alaska to southern California.
Notes: Since the Baetic olive burrows in the sand most of its life, it does not need to see. Thus it is not surprising that all species of *Olivella*, including this one, have no eyes. A similar species, the purple olive (above), is a wider and larger snail often found on the same beaches.

❯ WHITE BUBBLE SHELL

Haminoea vesicula

Other names: White bubble snail; blister glassy-bubble.
Description: Light brown; shaped somewhat like a slug with a thin shell covering a portion of the body.
Size: To ³/₄" (1.8 cm) high.
Habitat: On eel-grass and seaweed in muddy bays or sandy areas, intertidal zone. Also known to burrow just below surface of sand or mud.
Range: Alaska to Gulf of California.
Notes: The internal shell of this species is almost completely covered by its body. Its deep yellow egg ribbons can sometimes be found in July, on sandy bottom shores. If you are lucky enough to find a particularly light specimen of this species, it is possible to observe the pulsing of its heart through the shell.

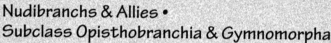

Nudibranchs & Allies •
Subclass Opisthobranchia & Gymnomorpha

The nudibranchs, or "sea slugs," are favorites of divers, beachcombers and snorkelers because many of them display such spectacular colors and patterns. Others have coloring that allows them to match their environment very closely. The nudibranch has a shell early in its life, but the shell is soon lost. Predators are few and far between. Many nudibranchs have chemical defenses or discharge stinging cells called nematocysts. All nudibranchs have a pair of intricate projections near the head, called rhinophores, which help them detect chemicals in the water. Some of these chemicals can help lead the nudibranch to food sources.

Subclass Opisthobranchia

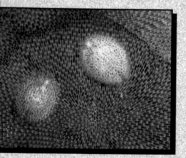

❯ CRYPTIC NUDIBRANCH

Doridella steinbergae

Other name: Steinberg's dorid.
Description: Color is a mixture of brown and white in an irregular grid pattern. Body is tiny and flat, closely resembling the bryozoan on which it feeds.
Size: To ⁵/₈" (1.7 cm) long.
Habitat: Usually found feeding on kelp encrusting bryozoan (see p. 127), low intertidal zone.
Range: Prince William Sound, Alaska to Baja California.
Notes: This nudibranch is easy to miss unless you are looking for it. Its only food source, the kelp encrusting bryozoan, lives on bull kelp (see p. 165) and a few other seaweeds. Check this bryozoan closely, as the tiny cryptic nudibranch spends most of its life there.

> RUFUS TIPPED NUDIBRANCH

Acanthodoris nanaimoensis

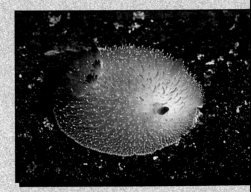

Other names: Nanaimo dorid; *Acanthodoris columbina.*
Description: White or gray body covered with yellow-tipped projections. Red tips grace the antennae-like rhinopores and edges of the gills.
Size: To 1¹/₈" (3 cm) long.
Habitat: Low intertidal zone to subtidal waters.
Range: Alaska to California.
Notes: There are two distinct color phases for this species. In the light phase the body is typically white overall, while the darker form is mottled with dark gray. In both phases, the distinctive yellow-tipped projections cover the entire body and red is present on the gills and the tips of the rhinopores. Bryozoans make up the diet of this species.

> BARNACLE-EATING DORID

Onchidoris bilamellata

Other names: Rough-mantled sea slug; formerly *Onchidoris fusca.*
Description: Color is a mixture of browns and cream colors. Blunt-tipped projections cover the entire body. The simple gills form a broad horseshoe.
Size: To ³/₄" (2 cm) long.
Habitat: On rocks on or near mud bottoms, low intertidal zone.
Range: Alaska to Baja California.
Notes: As its name suggests, barnacles are the only food of the adults of this species. (Juveniles feed on encrusting bryozoans.) The nudibranch sucks out the barnacle's body contents with a special pumping mechanism. This dorid is also found on both sides of the Atlantic coast.

›ORANGE-SPOTTED NUDIBRANCH
Triopha catalinae

Other names: Sea clown triopha; *Triopha carpenteri.*
Description: White, elongated body with bright orange or red tips on all projections. There are rhinophores and a circlet of branched gills.
Size: Normally to 2³/4" (7 cm) long, but can grow to 6" (15 cm) long.
Habitat: In tidepools and kelp beds, mid-intertidal zone to water 115' (35 m) deep.
Range: Alaska to Baja California.
Notes: This nudibranch and other species have been observed crawling upside down on the surface of tidepools. The individual can do this by secreting a trail of slime and moving along it. If it falls, it merely crawls back to resume its course. This nudibranch feeds on bryozoans.

›YELLOW-EDGED NUDIBRANCH
Cadlina luteomarginata

Other names: Yellow-edged cadlina; *Cadlina marginata.*
Description: White body edged with bright lemon-yellow trim. A ring of 6 frilly white gills tipped with yellow are located at the rear.
Size: To 3" (8 cm) long.
Habitat: Under ledges and rocks in tidepools, low tide to water 65' (20 m) deep.
Range: Alaska to Pt. Eugenia, Mexico.
Notes: The body of this beautiful nudibranch feels gritty or sandpaper-like because of the many sharp projections on its dorsal surface. The yellow-edged nudibranch feeds on a variety of sponge species.

>RED NUDIBRANCH
Rostanga pulchra

Other names: Crimson doris; red sponge nudibranch.
Description: Bright red or tan, similar in color to the red sponge on which it feeds. Small oval body, rounded in front and pointed toward the rear.
Size: To 1¹/8" (3 cm) long. Intertidal specimens tend to be much smaller.
Habitat: On rocky shores with overhanging ledges or large boulders, intertidal zone to water 30' (9 m) deep.
Range: Alaska to Mexico.
Notes: This common nudibranch is an excellent example of camouflage. It incorporates into its own body the pigment of the red sponges on which it feeds, which helps it to blend in to the red sponge substrate. Its egg masses are also vivid red and laid on sponges in spring or early summer, so that they too blend in with their substrate. Their whole life revolves around the red sponges on which they feed. Studies have shown that some individuals move about a great deal, while others are apparently much more sedentary. One individual was found on the same sponge it had been observed on 37 days earlier.

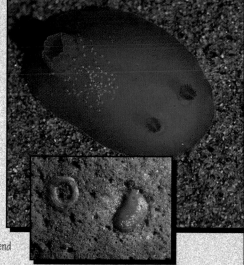

This red nudibranch has laid its circular egg case on red encrusting sponge *Ophlitaspongia pennata*, its food source.

• •

>MONTEREY DORID
Archidoris montereyensis

Other name: Monterey sea lemon.
Description: Flat body, shaped somewhat like a slice of lemon with **small black spots covering some of its small rounded body projections**. Two horn-like rhinophores at front; cluster of yellowish-brown gills at rear.
Size: To 2³/4" (7 cm) long on average, occasionally to 4³/4" (12 cm) long.
Habitat: On rocky shorelines, intertidal zones to water 160' (49 m) deep.
Range: Alaska to San Diego, California.
Notes: The Monterey dorid lays its eggs on rock, year round. Each spiral-shaped cluster may contain up to 2 million eggs. The bread crumb sponge (see p. 24) is the primary food and this dorid can often be found there. A similar species, the sea lemon (below), can be distinguished by the black spots between the small projection tips on its back or dorsal side.

A group of three adults out of water with their egg cases.

• •

⟩ SEA LEMON
Anisodoris nobilis

Other names: Noble Pacific doris; speckled sea lemon.

Description: Flat, bright yellow to orange body covered dorsally with short rounded projections with **black spots between the projections**. A pair of pointed rhinophores at head region, a pair of frilly white gills at rear.

Size: Usually to 4" (10 cm) long, but occasionally to 10" (26 cm).

Habitat: Low intertidal zone to water 750' (229 m) deep.

Range: Kodiak Island, Alaska to Baja California.

Notes: This common nudibranch feeds on several types of encrusting sponges. Many nudibranchs have a distinctive smell, which indicates the importance of smell to this group of invertebrates. The sea lemon has a somewhat fruity odor which may help repel predators. Like other dorids, this one has a flattened body and lacks large projections (cerata) along its body. The gills are usually seen as a rosette on the animal's back.

⟩ RINGED NUDIBRANCH
Diaulula sandiegensis

Other names: Spotted nudibranch; ringed doris; brown-spotted nudibranch; leopard nudibranch; San Diego dorid; ring-spotted nudibranch.

Description: Light brown to gray with various sizes of brown rings or spots distributed randomly over the body. A pair of white antennae in head region, a pair of frilly gills at rear.

Size: Normally to 2¾" (7 cm) long, but has been known to grow to 4" (10 cm).

Habitat: Under rocks, ledges and kelp, low intertidal zone to subtidal waters 110' (34 m) deep.

Range: Alaska to Mexico.

Notes: The ringed nudibranch feeds on intertidal and subtidal sponges. An overhanging rock ledge is a typical location where this animal lays its white spiral of eggs—up to 16 million of them. Northern specimens are generally darker and have more rings or spots on their body than those from the south.

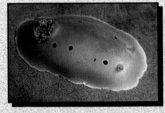

Darker colored individual.

>FROSTED NUDIBRANCH
Dirona albolineata

Other names: Alabaster nudibranch; white-streaked dirona; white-lined dirona; chalk-lined dirona.
Description: Opaque, with projections that are leaf-like and edged with a fine, brilliant white line.
Size: Normally to 1½" (4 cm), but can grow to 7" (18 cm) long.
Habitat: On rocky shores, low intertidal zone to water 100' (30 m) deep.
Range: Alaska to California.

The purple-tinged color phase of the frosted nudibranch.

Notes: This nudibranch feeds on small snails by cracking the shells with its powerful jaws. Other foods include sea anemones, sea squirts and bryozoans. The frosted nudibranch is often found during very low tides. It occurs in three color phases: white, purple-tinged and orange-tinged.

>OPALESCENT NUDIBRANCH
Hermissenda crassicornis

Other names: Hermissenda nudibranch; thick-horned nudibranch; long-horned nudibranch; *Phidiana crassicornis*.
Description: Colorful yellow-green body, orange areas on the back and a clear blue line on the sides. White tips of the projections (cerata) contain stinging cells (nematocysts) ingested by eating hydroids.
Size: Normally to 1½" (4 cm) long, but can grow to 3" (8 cm) long.
Habitat: On mud flats, eel-grass beds, docks and rocky intertidal areas.
Range: Alaska to Mexico.
Notes: This nudibranch feeds on hydroids, sea squirts, ascidians, other mollusks, various types of eggs and pieces of fish. It is an aeolid, a type of nudibranch with many projections (cerata) along its body. The center of these appendages are responsible for digestion, while the surface is necessary for respiration. Because aeolids feed on hydroids and anemones, which have stinging cells (nematocysts), these cells may become attached to the nudibranch's cerata, and act as defenses against the nudibranch's enemies.

The opalescent nudibranch is a common and docile-looking creature which is considered to be a voracious, ill-natured and cannibalistic member of the nudibranch family. It has a life span of not much more than 4 months. Egg clusters can often be found in the area where adults are observed.

> SHAGGY MOUSE NUDIBRANCH
Aeolidia papillosa

Shaggy mouse nudibranch and eggs in tidepool.

Other names: Shag-rug nudibranch; maned nudibranch; papillose aeolid.

Description: Whitish or pinkish body with gray or brown spots. Many colorless or gray-brown projections (cerata), typically with a bald spot down the middle.

Size: To 2³/4" (7 cm) long.

Habitat: On protected rocky shores, sandy beaches and in eel-grass beds, intertidal zone to water 2,200' (671 m) deep.

Range: Alaska to southern California.

Notes: Sea anemones, including the plumose anemone (see p. 40) and the aggregating anemone (p. 35), provide food for this appropriately named nudibranch. It feeds at least once a day, consuming up to 100 percent of its body weight. In order for the shaggy mouse nudibranch to feed on anemones, it must first become immune to the stinging properties of the stinging cells (nematocysts) on the anemone's tentacles. Apparently the nudibranch first touches the anemone, then retreats, which activates the production of a coating resistant to the stinging effects. The nudibranch can then feed on the anemone without becoming a meal itself.

Subclass Gymnomorpha

> LEATHER LIMPET
Onchidella borealis

Other name: Northwest onchidella.

Description: Variable in color from black or brown to gray, often with dots and streaks. Short tentacles with eyes on the tips. Body shape gives it the appearance of a limpet.

Size: To ¹/2" (1.2 cm) long.

Habitat: On seaweed and rocks, high to low intertidal zones.

Range: Alaska to northern California.

Notes: Although this common species resembles a limpet, it is actually closely related to the nudibranch (a nudibranch "ally"). However, it is almost terrestrial (prefers to be above the water), unlike true nudibranchs. Groups of several leather limpets are often found. They feed by scraping diatoms from rocks and algae when the tide goes out. The eyes of this species are at the tips of its tentacles. It lacks gills and may seek out trapped air bubbles from which to breathe while underwater.

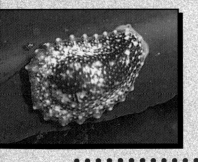

Bivalves • Class Bivalvia

Bivalves are a large group of animals each of which is covered by a pair of shells (valves). There are some 10,000 species of bivalves worldwide, including mussels, oysters, clams, scallops and shipworms. Some live in fresh water, but the majority are found in salt water environments, buried in sand and mud (clams), rock (piddocks) and wood (shipworms). Others have evolved to become mobile and capable of swimming (scallops). Bivalves have come to occupy very diverse environments, but remain relatively unchanged through time.

The world's largest bivalve, from the Indo-Pacific, grows to 5' (1.5 m) long and can weigh as much as 650 lbs (295 kg). Locally, the Pacific geoduck (see p. 99) can weigh up to 20 lbs (9 kg), while other species are as small as 1/16" (2 mm) wide. Clams feed, breathe and expel wastes through siphons, special tubes that extend from the clam to the surface. The siphons range from very short, as in the Nuttall's cockle (p. 91), to 3' (1 m) long, as in the Pacific geoduck. Many species of bivalves have been, and continue to be, utilized for food.

>CALIFORNIA MUSSEL

Mytilus californianus

Other names: Surf mussel; sea mussel; ribbed mussel.
Description: Thin blue-black periostracum (covering) over shells. Exterior often has streak of brown. A series of **rounded ridges extend the length of each shell**.
Size: To 10" (25 cm) long.
Habitat: On exposed rocky shores, mid-intertidal zone to depths of 330' (100 m).
Range: Alaska to Mexico.
Notes: This species has a high reproduction capability: 100,000 eggs can be produced annually by one female. The California mussel can grow 3 1/2" (9 cm) in one year's time. It also has many predators, including sea stars, predaceous snails, crabs, gulls, sea otters and humans. Aboriginal people of the west coast used this species extensively, its flesh for food and its shells for implements. A similar species, the Pacific blue mussel (below), is smaller and lacks the rounded ridges.

⟩PACIFIC BLUE MUSSEL

Mytilus trossulus

Other names: Edible mussel; blue mussel; bay mussel; formerly (and incorrectly) *Mytilus edulis*.

Description: Color varies from blue or brown to black. Distinctive **smooth, wedge-shaped shells**.

Size: Can grow to 4½" (11 cm) long but is usually much smaller.

Habitat: In somewhat sheltered areas, mid-intertidal zone to subtidal water 132' (40 m) deep.

Range: Alaska to Mexico.

Notes: This mussel produces a sticky substance which hardens into thread-like fibers, the byssus, with which the mussel attaches to substrates such as rocks. If you try to remove a mussel from its bed, you will discover how strong these fibers can be. Mussels feed on plankton by pumping up to 3 quarts (3 L) of sea water per hour through their gills. This flow is generated by the rhythmic movement of tiny hairs (cilia). When the tide goes out, mussels close their shells tight to stop from drying out. This species has been studied extensively, and its former scientific name *Mytilus edulis* has been recently revised due to results of electrophoretic studies (a specialized technique of measuring suspended particles moving in fluid toward an electrode). Other mussels have been introduced and are hybridizing with this species.

⟩NORTHERN HORSEMUSSEL

Modiolus modiolus

Other names: Bearded mussel; horse mussel; *Volsella modiolus*.

Description: Brown to purplish-black shells with thin skin-like covering (periostracum).

Size: To 7" (18 cm) long.

Habitat: Often partially buried in gravel or rocks, intertidal zone to depths of 660' (200 m).

Range: Bering Sea to Monterey, California.

Notes: Unlike most mussels, northern horsemussels can burrow, and often cluster together in groups. Their thread-like fibers (byssus) attach to the surrounding rock and to their buddies, aiding them to stay in place. This mussel is circumpolar in distribution. It is not considered a gourmet item.

>CALIFORNIA DATEMUSSEL
Adula californiensis

Other names: California pea-pod borer; pea pod borer; *Botula californiensis.*
Description: Shiny chocolate-brown shell covering (periostracum). Shells elongated with fine hair-like threads at basal end.
Size: To 1¼" (3.2 cm) long.
Habitat: In clay and soft rock, intertidal zone to depths of 66' (20 m).
Range: Vancouver Island to San Diego, California.
Notes: This mussel's shells are very fragile. It is an uncommon species that can sometimes be found at the same sites as other rock-boring bivalves. Scientists know little of its biology.

• •

>OLYMPIA OYSTER
Ostrea conchaphila

Other names: Native Pacific oyster; California oyster; *Ostrea lurida.*
Description: Small gray oyster with **round to elongated shells**.
Size: To 3½" (8.8 cm) in diameter.
Habitat: At a variety of sites, including tidepools and estuaries with mud or gravel flats, intertidal zone to depths of 165' (50 m). Solid objects such as rocks are required for this species to attach.
Range: Sitka, Alaska to Panama.
Notes: This native species is capable of changing its sex during spawning season. Like several others species, this oyster is called a protandrous hermaphrodite. It is never totally male or female, but alternates between male and female phases. The female then holds the young inside her mantle until their shells are developed. While the young develop, the male gonads begin the process of producing sperm. And so the phases alternate. Because of pollution, overharvesting and the species' slow growth (it requires 4 to 6 years to mature), its populations have declined sharply. A similar species, the introduced Pacific oyster (below), is a larger oyster with a fluted edge to its shells.

• •

> PACIFIC OYSTER
Crassostrea gigas

Other names: Japanese oyster; giant Pacific oyster.
Description: Gray to white shells with purple to black new growth. **Irregular shape with fluted exterior edge.** Lower shell is cup-shaped and larger than top shell.
Size: To 12" (30 cm) long.
Habitat: Intertidal zone to depths of 20' (6 m).
Range: Alaska to California.
Notes: The Pacific oyster was introduced to BC and Washington in 1922. It can be harvested commercially after only 2 to 4 years but is known to live longer than 20 years. If you are harvesting this oyster, leave the shells on the beach. They provide attachment sites for new generations of oysters. Harvesters should possess a license and be aware of bag limits and closures, especially for red tide (PSP) (see p. 17).

> GREEN FALSE-JINGLE
Pododesmus macroschisma

Other names: Rock oyster; jingle shell; false Pacific jingle shell; pearly monia; formerly *Pododesmus cepio*; occasionally misspelled as *P. machrochisma*.
Description: Gray-white upper shell with radiating light lines and iridescent green interior. Lower shell is smaller and flat with a large hole in the middle.
Size: To 5¹/₈" (13 cm) long.
Habitat: Attached to solid objects, low intertidal zone to depths of 300' (90 m).
Range: Alaska to Baja California.
Notes: This species is edible, though it is not an abundant intertidal species. The bright orange mantle is sometimes visible when the shells are open. Its distinctive shells are often washed up on beaches. Its name likely originates from the sound the shells make jingling in a beachcomber's pocket.

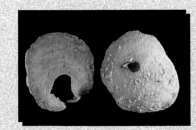

⟩Smooth Pink Scallop

Chlamys rubida

Other names: Swimming scallop; reddish scallop.
Description: Pink or purple to yellow shells, circular with triangular bases. Many **smooth ribs** radiate from each base. 2 uneven flanges or "ears" are situated on each base.
Size: To 2¹/₂" (6.6 cm) high.
Habitat: In rocky areas, at depths of 3–660' (1–200 m).
Range: Alaska to San Diego, California.
Notes: Tidepools do not harbor this scallop, but while walking the beach you may find shells of this beautiful species on the sand. Living specimens are often encrusted with sponges. This scallop and the spiny pink scallop (see below) are harvested by commercial and recreational fishermen. The taste of fresh scallops is hard to beat!

⟩Spiny Pink Scallop

Chlamys hastata

Other names: Pink scallop; Pacific pink scallop; *Chlamys hericia.*
Description: Purple to orange shells, nearly circular, with triangular base bearing 2 uneven "ears." Numerous **spiny ribs** radiate from base.
Size: To 3¹/₄" (8.3 cm) in diameter.
Habitat: In rocky areas, at depths of 7–500' (2–150 m).
Range: Alaska to San Diego, California.
Notes: This scallop is larger and more abundant than the smooth pink scallop (above). It is not found in the intertidal zone but its distinctive shells are sometimes found washed up on sandy, exposed beaches. This species is often covered in encrusting sponges. The spiny pink scallop reaches maturity at 2 years and lives to 6 years. The sexes are separate, with females possessing orange ovaries and males white testes.

▷ GIANT ROCK SCALLOP
Crassadoma gigantea

Other names: Purple-hinged rock scallop; *Hinnites giganteus, Hinnites multirugosus.*
Description: Shell color varies from brown to green and is often obscured by myriad encrusting species. Round, thick shells with deep purple color on inside hinges. When shells are open, mantle is visible—usually bright orange and lined with many tiny blue eyes.
Size: To 10" (25 cm) in diameter.
Habitat: In rocky areas, low intertidal zone to depths of 150' (45 m).
Range: Alaska to Baja California.
Notes: This is a free swimming species until it reaches approximately 1" (2.5 cm) in diameter. At that time it usually attaches to a rock or shell where it remains for the rest of its life. Older individuals are often found with encrusting algae or boring sponges growing on the shells. The giant rock scallop can live as long as 50 years. This species, like all scallops, is a gourmet item. If you harvest it, ensure that you are aware of area closures, bag limits and any protected areas where harvesting is not allowed.

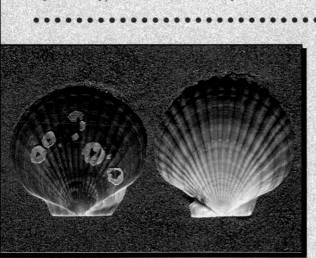

▷ WEATHERVANE SCALLOP
Patinopecten caurinus

Other names: Giant Pacific scallop; *Pecten caurinus.*
Description: Reddish-brown upper shell, yellowish lower shell. Large, nearly circular shells with up to 24 ribs radiating from the bottom.
Size: To 11" (28 cm) in diameter.
Habitat: Normally found on sand or gravel bottoms at depths of 33–660' (10–200 m).
Range: Alaska to Point Sur, California.
Notes: This species is the largest living scallop in the world. It is not normally found in the intertidal zone, but during winter storms it can be unwillingly deposited, in large numbers, on surf-swept beaches. These stranded animals sometimes accumulate, lying stranded until the next tide takes them back into the ocean. Barnacles are often attached to the top sholl of this impressive scallop.

> # NUTTALL'S COCKLE
Clinocardium nuttallii

Other names: Cockle; basket cockle; heart cockle; *Cardium corbis.*
Description: Shell color varies from light brown with mottling in young individuals to much darker in older specimens. Shells are roughly oval with **heart-shaped cross-section**, prominent radiating ribs on exterior.
Size: Occasionally to 5¹/₂" (14 cm) long.
Habitat: On both sand and mud beaches, midintertidal zone to subtidal depth of 80' (24 m).
Range: Bering Sea, Alaska to San Diego, California.

Notes: This cockle has been known to live 16 years. Breeding may take place at 2 years. Since its siphons are very short, this species is usually found on or near the surface of tidal flats. Predatory sea stars such as the giant pink star (see p. 134) and the sunflower star (p. 135) are among this clam's predators. The Nuttall's cockle uses its long foot in a remarkable thrusting motion—pole-vault style—to push off its enemies.

• •

> # FAT GAPER
Tresus capax

Other names: Gaper clam; horse clam; horseneck clam; rubberneck clam; blue clam; Washington clam; *Schizothoerus capax.*
Description: Brown to black shell covering (periostracum). **Shells are oval.** Tips of siphons vary from green to black in color.
Size: To 3.3 lbs (1.5 kg) in weight, to 10" (25 cm) long.
Habitat: Normally in mixtures of mud, sand and gravel, mid-intertidal zone to depths of 100' (33 m).

Range: Kodiak Island, Alaska to northern California.
Notes: Several clam species, including the fat gaper, announce their presence by spouting a geyser as they retract their siphons in the sand. This is the sign to collectors that they have discovered a clam bed, but fat gapers are known for being tough to dig out. The aboriginal people of the west coast also found this clam difficult to collect because of its ability to bury itself as far down as 20" (50 cm). When collected, the clams were steamed in pits and their shells used as cups or ladles.

• •

⟩ PACIFIC GAPER
Tresus nuttallii

Other names: Summer clam; rubberneck clam; big-neck clam; horse clam; otter-shell clam; great Washington clam; *Schizothoerus nuttalli*.
Description: White to yellowish shells, brown to black shell covering (periostracum), which peels easily. Noticeably **oval-elongated shells**. Tip of siphon is tan to yellowish-orange.
Size: To 4 lbs (1.8 kg), to 8" (20 cm) long.
Habitat: In sandy areas, intertidal zone to depths of 165' (50 m). Can burrow as deep as 36" (90 cm) into the sand.
Range: BC to Baja California.
Notes: This clam is noted for sporadically spurting jets of water approximately 3' (1 m) into the air. It is believed to be a summer spawner. Usually it is found deeper in the sand and lower on the beach than the similar fat gaper (above), and the fat gaper has broader, rounder shells. Native people of the Northwest Coast dried the siphons of both of these species for winter food.

A siphon "show."

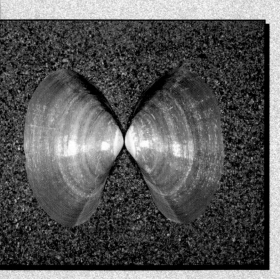

⟩ HOOKED SURFCLAM
Simomactra falcata

Other name: *Spisula falcata*.
Description: White shells with smooth, thin, shiny brown covering (periostracum). Hinge is close to the rear.
Size: To 3½" (9 cm) in length.
Habitat: In protected bays and similar areas, low intertidal zone to depths of 165' (50 m).
Range: Queen Charlotte Islands, BC to Baja California.
Notes: This clam builds a shallow burrow in the sand. It can close its shells tightly when required. Its thin, shiny shells are always a welcome sight to beachwalkers, as it is not commonly found.

>Pacific Razor-clam
Siliqua patula

Other name: Razor clam.
Description: Yellow to yellowish-brown shells with glossy, smooth finish. Oval and flattened in shape. Foot and siphon are buff-colored.
Size: To 6" (15 cm) long, 2³/8" (6 cm) wide.
Habitat: On surf-swept sandy beaches, low intertidal zone to subtidal waters. Digs to depths of 24" (60 cm).
Range: Alaska to central California.

Notes: This clam is very active and has been observed to bury itself completely in sand in less than 7 seconds. To do so, the clam pushes its foot deeper into the sand while its fluids are displaced. The tip of the foot then expands, forming an anchor. Then, as the foot contracts, the animal draws deeper into the sand. Individuals have been known to live to 18 years of age. In the north, breeding probably occurs in July and August. Pacific razor-clams were traditionally gathered in May and June, at low spring tides, by Native people. Today they are collected by both recreational and commercial fishermen. If you collect this species, be sure that the area is safe from red tide or PSP (see p. 17).

- - -

>Bodega Tellin
Tellina bodegensis

Other name: Bodega clam.
Description: White elongated shells with polished surfaces and very fine concentric lines on exterior. Interior is white, often with a tint of yellow or pink.
Size: To 2³/8" (6 cm) long.
Habitat: On exposed beaches, intertidal zone to depths of 300' (91 m).
Range: Sitka, Alaska to Gulf of California.
Notes: This is an uncommon species but its distinctive shells are sometimes found washed up on the beach. The bodega tellin has two separate siphons which extend to the surface. It is reportedly an excellent tasting clam, but is too scarce to be harvested regularly.

›BALTIC MACOMA
Macoma balthica

Other names: Tiny pink clam; *Macoma inconspicua*.
Description: Oval shells are often pink but can also be blue, orange or yellow.
Size: To 1½" (4 cm) long.
Habitat: In areas with mixed mud and sand, mud flats and eel-grass beds, intertidal zone to depths of 130' (39 m).
Range: Beaufort Sea to San Francisco Bay, California.
Notes: This common species is often found to be plentiful in muddy areas. It

also lives in northern Atlantic waters. Members of the genus *Macoma* have two separate siphons, one for water to enter and the other for it to leave. The siphons extend to the surface for these species to feed, breathe and expel waste.

›EXPANDED MACOMA
Macoma expansa

Other name: Formerly *Macoma liotricha*.
Description: White to yellowish. Smooth, thin oval shells have a polished covering (periostracum) on exterior.
Size: To 2" (5 cm) long.
Habitat: In sand in both protected and exposed sites, intertidal zone to water 100' (30 m) deep.
Range: Alaska to southern Baja California.
Notes: The shells of the expanded macoma tend to be slightly more elongated in the southern portion of its range, less elongated in the northern portion. Finding a fragile shell of this species on a beach is always a treat.

›Bent-nose Macoma

Macoma nasuta

Other name: Bent-nosed clam.
Description: Thin, brown, wrinkled shell covering (periostracum). The clam gets its name from its shells, which are noticeably curved to the right.
Size: To 2" (5 cm) long.
Habitat: In protected areas with mud and sand, intertidal zone to 130' (39 m). Can burrow 4–6" (10–15 cm) below the surface.
Range: Alaska to Baja California.

Notes: This clam typically lies flat with its "nose" pointed upward, which allows its siphons to reach the surface. Shells from this species have been found in many middens in the Northwest Coast area. Lewis's moonsnail (see p. 72) is known to be an important predator of this clam.

- -

›Dark Mahogany-clam

Nuttallia obscurata

Other name: Varnish clam.
Description: Rich brown shell covering (periostracum) with polished finish. Thin, round shells with white to rich purple interior.
Size: To 2¼" (5.5 cm) long.

Habitat: In sand, high to mid-intertidal zones. Burrows quickly to a depth of 8" (20 cm).
Range: Barkeley Sound, Strait of Georgia, BC, south to the San Juan Islands, Washington.
Notes: This clam was introduced from Japan, possibly as early as 1980. Since that time, it has spread through the Strait of Georgia and south to the San Juan Islands.

- -

> BUTTER CLAM
Saxidomus gigantea

Other names: Washington clam; smooth Washington clam; formerly *Saxidomus giganteus*.

Description: Shell color changes from yellowish in young specimens to white or gray in older individuals. In areas with mud, shells can be stained black by iron sulphate. Shells are oval, etched with many concentric lines centered at the hinge.

Size: To 6" (15 cm) long.

Habitat: On sheltered sand and gravel beaches, low intertidal zone to water 60' (18 m) deep. Burrow can reach a depth of 14" (35 cm).

Range: Aleutian Islands, Alaska to California.

Notes: This species has been known to live for more than 20 years. It also has a long history of commercial use. To collect it, first ensure that the area is safe from red tide (PSP) and pollution. PSP toxins accumulate particularly in the dark tips of the siphons of the butter clam, so remove them before eating your catch, just to be extra safe.

> PACIFIC LITTLENECK
Protothaca staminea

Other names: Rock cockle; rock venus; rock clam; hardshell clam.

Description: White to light brown shells, often with fine irregular brown pattern. Generally **round shells** with both radiating and concentric raised lines. **Rough texture on inside margin of shell.**

Size: To 3" (7.5 cm) long.

Habitat: On sand and gravel beaches, mid-intertidal zone to water 60' (18 m) deep. Can burrow to a depth of approximately 4" (10 cm).

Range: Aleutian Islands, Alaska to southern California.

Notes: This clam is generally slow-growing, reaching legal harvestable size in 3 to 4 years but living as long as 16 years. Breeding occurs during the summer months, after a maturation period of 3 to 5 years. A similar species, the Japanese littleneck (see below), has more elongated shells. The Pacific littleneck is excellent eating when steamed. But you must have a sport fishing license to harvest them legally, and be sure to check with local officials to ensure the clams are safe to eat in the area you wish to harvest from.

> JAPANESE LITTLENECK

Venerupis philippinarum

Other names: Manila clam; Japanese littleneck clam; formerly *Tapes philippinarum; Tapes japonica.*
Description: Light brown to gray shells, often with patterns of streaks and blotches of darker browns. **Oval-elongated shells** with both radiating and concentric raised lines. **Smooth inside margin of shell.** Interior often touched with purple.
Size: To 3" (7.5 cm) long.
Habitat: In muddy gravel, high intertidal to shallow subtidal zones. Burrows to depth of approximately 4" (10 cm).
Range: Central BC to California.
Notes: This species was accidentally introduced to North America with the seed of Pacific oysters. It appears to be unable to withstand extreme temperature changes, as mass winter mortalities have been noted. This species requires only 2 years to reach legal harvestable size of 2" (5.1 cm). If you plan to harvest Japanese littlenecks, check with officials to ensure that the area is free from pollution and red tide.

Japanese littleneck (left) and Pacific littleneck (right).

> CALIFORNIA SOFTSHELL-CLAM

Cryptomya californica

Other names: False mya; California glass mya.
Description: White or off-white oval shells with brown covering (periostracum) and a series of concentric rings.
Size: To 1¼" (3.2 cm) long.
Habitat: In sand and mud in the intertidal zone, to water 265' (80 m) deep. Burrows to depths of 20" (50 cm).
Range: Alaska to Peru.
Notes: The siphons of this small clam are only ¹/₁₆" (1 mm) long, unusually short for a clam. This species lives deeper in the sand than its siphons would normally allow by utilizing the burrows of the blue mud shrimp (see p. 111) or the bay ghost shrimp (p. 112). Here, adjacent to these deeper burrows, it is able to feed from their circulating water by using its short siphon.

97

›SOFTSHELL-CLAM
Mya arenaria

Other names: Mud clam; soft clam.
Description: White or gray shells with yellow or brown covering (periostracum). Shells are relatively soft (as clam's name implies) and slightly elongated with many concentric rings. Large spoon-shaped projection (chondrophore) at hinge of one shell.
Size: To 4" (10 cm) long.

A young softshell-clam.

Habitat: Buried in sand and mud in estuaries, intertidal zones. Burrows to a depth of approximately 8" (20 cm).
Range: Queen Charlotte Islands, BC to California.

The distinctive shell interior with its chondrophore.

Notes: The softshell-clam burrows in mud and sand in a unique way. Water is ejected below the clam, pushing sand out of the way and enabling it to move deeper. This slow method of burrowing is more effective in sand than in mud. This clam also has a special sac off the stomach which holds a food reserve. Species is believed to have been accidentally introduced to North America in the last century. Its shells are not found in the middens of Native people, which supports this theory.

›BORING SOFTSHELL-CLAM
Platyodon cancellatus

Other names: Chubby mya; checked softshell-clam; checked borer.
Description: Yellow-brown shell covering (periostracum) overlays rectangular shells. Narrow, bony projection inside one shell near the hinge.
Size: To 3" (7.6 cm) long.
Habitat: Species builds an elongated burrow in soft rock or clay to 5" (13 cm) deep, often with sand covering the entrance. Intertidal zone to subtidal waters 330' (100 m) deep.
Range: Queen Charlotte Islands, BC to Baja California.
Notes: This clam can bore directly into soft rock by shell movement rather than a rotating motion. It does so by alternate contractions of muscles in the shells, which causes the shells to rock. As a result, it can bore holes that closely match the shape of its shells, rather than the round holes of other boring species. It is also reported to have been found boring into low-grade concrete. Historically, this clam was harvested by the Haida people on the Queen Charlotte Islands of BC.

>Pacific Geoduck
Panope abrupta

Other names: King clam; gooeyduck; *Panopea generosa.*

Description: Gray shells with yellow covering (periostracum). Shells are heavy and oblong with concentric rings. Body and immense siphons cannot be completely contained within shells. Tip of siphon, when viewed from above, is light brown, without tentacles or pads.

Size: Shells to 9" (23 cm) long; most are much smaller. Largest recorded weight is 20 lbs (9 kg).

Habitat: In protected beaches of gravel, sand and mud, intertidal zone to subtidal waters 200' (61 m) deep.

Range: Arctic Ocean to Panama.

Notes: This remarkable clam can extend its siphon nearly 3' (1 m) to the surface, and as a result it is not easily collected. Because the siphon is too large to be retracted completely into the shell, the geoduck relies on its deep burrow for protection. The giant pink star (see p. 134) feeds on the siphons of this clam by grasping them with its sticky tube feet. The Pacific geoduck is the largest burrowing clam in the world. It is also extensively harvested commercially. The total number of eggs produced by a single female during one year has been calculated to exceed 50 million; few of these survive, but individuals of this species have been known to live longer than 140 years.

>Arctic Hiatella
Hiatella arctica

Other names: Gallic saxicave; little gaper; red nose; *Hiatella gallicana.*

Description: Chalky white shells with rough, round-elongated shape. Red or orange siphon tips.

Size: To 2" (5 cm) long.

Habitat: Intertidal zone to subtidal waters 2,640' (800 m) deep.

Range: Alaska to Chile.

Notes: The Arctic hiatella bores into soft, uniform rock using a rocking motion. This species is also an opportunist, often moving into the burrows of other boring clams. Adults can attach directly to rock surfaces with weak byssus threads. The mottled star (see p. 133) is a known predator of this species.

› ROUGH PIDDOCK
Zirfaea pilsbryi

Other name: Pilsbry's piddock, *Zirphaea pilsbryi* (misspelled).

Description: White shells with brown covering (periostracum). Shells are roughly oval with rough concentric growth rings, and teeth developed at anterior end. **Shell exterior is divided into 2 separate sections** and gapes at both ends.

Size: To 6" (15 cm) long; siphon can extend to almost 12" (30 cm) long and 2" (5.1 cm) in diameter when extended.

Habitat: Species burrows into shale and clay, intertidal zone to subtidal depths of 412' (125 m).

Range: Bering Sea to Baja California.

Notes: The rough piddock rasps away at clay or soft rock to build its burrow with sharp tooth-like projections at the rear of the shells. As it digs it rotates, carving a circular burrow. This clam is a true "prisoner in its

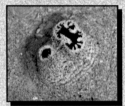

A siphon "show."

Detail of the rough piddock's cutting surface.

castle": it is embedded in its home until it dies. The rough piddock has been known to live 8 years. A similar rock-boring species, the flat-tip piddock (see below), has each shell divided into 3 sections.

› FLAT-TIP PIDDOCK
Penitella penita

Other names: Common piddock; formerly *Pholadidea penita*.

Description: Gray to brown shell covering (periostracum). Hinge is near one end of the 2 shells. **Wedge-shaped shells with exteriors divided into 3 separate sections.** Central near-triangular section separates the other 2 sections.

Size: To 3" (7.6 cm) long.

Habitat: Buried to 20" (50 cm) deep in soft rock, mud or hard clay, intertidal zone to water 72' (22 m) deep.

Range: Alaska to Baja California.

Notes: This piddock lives in burrows with only the siphon exposed to obtain food. The opening in the rock is typically small, since the clam begins to burrow when it is quite small. Burrowing is accomplished by simple mechanical abrasion of the rock by the shell. Since the animal is continually growing, it must continually enlarge its burrow. Once it has reached its full size, its foot is no longer required; the foot degenerates and the shells overgrow it. The similar rough piddock (see above) is a larger species with its exterior divided into 2 sections.

>SHIPWORM
Bankia setacea

Other names: Teredo; Pacific shipworm; feathery shipworm.
Description: Superficially a worm-like creature with small shells at the front end and 2 feather-like pallets or appendages at the rear.
Size: To 39" (1 m) long, 1" (2.5 cm) in diameter.
Habitat: Species bores into wood, intertidal zone to subtidal water 300' (90 m) deep.
Range: Bering Sea to Gulf of California.

Notes: The young of the shipworm (veligers) look like miniature clams in the first stages of development. Changes occur once they settle on a wood source to begin their "boring" life. They use the teeth on their shells to rasp away at the wood while they burrow. The 2 feather-like appendages that grace the rear can be used to stopper their burrow. Both wood and plankton provide food as this bivalve grows. Considerable damage to untreated wood is caused by this species annually.

• •

>ROCK ENTODESMA
Entodesma navicula

Other names: Rock-dwelling entodesma; rock-dwelling clam; northwest ugly clam; *Entodesma saxicola*; *Agriodesma saxicola*.
Description: Brown shell covering (periostracum) which usually cracks when dried out. This cracking often breaks the shell as well. Shell is usually oblong but often shaped by its habitat.

Size: To 6" (15 cm) long.
Habitat: Along shores covered with broken rocks, among rock crevices, intertidal zone to depth of 65' (20 m).
Range: Aleutian Islands, Alaska to southern California.
Notes: The young of this species look much different than adult specimens. A light brown periostracum completely covers the shell of the young, giving it a unique appearance. As this species is sometimes called the northwest ugly clam, you know it is not one of our prettier shells to collect.

The shell of a young individual.

Octopods & Squids • Class Cephalopoda

This group of mollusks have several remarkable characteristics. A total of 8 or more arms are positioned around the mouth, and 2 gills, 2 kidneys and 3 hearts are also present. A dark fluid is produced in some species, which can be released to aid in defense against predators.

▷ GIANT PACIFIC OCTOPUS
Octopus dofleini

Other name: Pacific octopus.
Description: Color varies from reddish to brownish, with possible color changes according to mood and background color. Prominent skin folds.
Size: Arms spread to 10' (3 m) across. At least one individual measured 32' (9.6 m) across, but the beachcomber can expect to see intertidal specimens reaching to 5' (1.5 m) across.
Habitat: In tidepools and rocky areas, low intertidal zone to subtidal waters 1,650' (503 m) deep.
Range: Alaska to southern California.
Notes: This octopus is the largest in the world, with one individual recorded at a weight of nearly 600 lbs (272 kg). The giant Pacific octopus is often shy by nature or inquisitive. It is well known for its rapid color changes, caused by the presence of large pigmentation cells which can match the color of the animal's background. This octopus is known to live to 5 years. If you find it on the beach, **do not pick it up**. It can deliver a nasty bite.

A giant Pacific octopus moves in the intertidal zone.

LAMPSHELLS Phylum Brachiopoda

▷ COMMON LAMPSHELL
Terebratalia transversa

Other names: Common Pacific brachiopod; lampshell.
Description: Color varies from gray to pinkish. Short stalk supports the hinged shells, which may or may not be ribbed.
Size: To 1" (2.5 cm) wide.
Habitat: On rocks, low intertidal zone to subtidal waters 6,000' (1,829 m) deep.
Range: Alaska to Baja California.
Notes: This brachiopod is often thought to resemble an Aladdin's lamp, hence its name. Its chief enemies are crabs, which have learned that by chipping away at its shell, they will eventually reach the tender meal inside. Fortunately for the common lampshell, it is usually attached to a rock in a covered or hidden location. A full 10 years is required for this brachiopod to reach its maximum size.

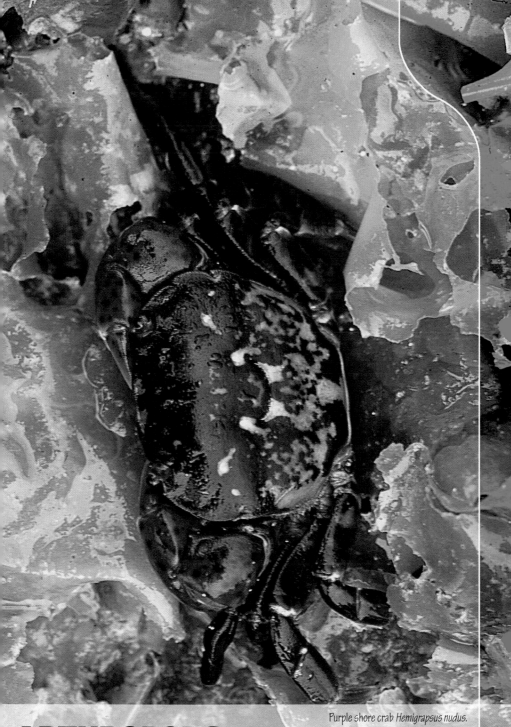

Purple shore crab *Hemigrapsus nudus*.

ARTHROPODS
Phylum Arthropoda

Arthropods are acclaimed to be the most widespread group of creatures in the animal kingdom, as well as having the greatest number of species. Marine arthropods include barnacles, isopods, amphipods, shrimps and crabs. All members of this large group, phylum Arthropoda, have "jointed limbs" and an exoskeleton, or a skeleton that covers their body like armor.

Barnacles • Class Cirripedia

Barnacles have modified legs (cirri) which sweep through the water like a net to collect tiny planktonic food. They reach sexual maturity at approximately 80 days and their reproduction is unusual. Males may become females and vice versa at any time. To reproduce, the male must locate a female close enough for his penis to reach, as barnacles are unable to move from their substrate. The penis, however, can reach up to 20 times the length of the barnacle's body.

›THATCHED BARNACLE

Semibalanus cariosus

Other name: formerly *Balanus cariosus*.
Description: Immature specimens and uncrowded groups are normally white, older individuals or crowded colonies are grayish. Many downward-pointing spines normally cover the steep walls. Base is membranous.
Size: To 1½" (4 cm) in diameter, 2³/8" (6 cm) high.
Habitat: Attached to rock, mid-intertidal zone.
Range: Alaska to southern California.
Notes: The spines covering the walls of this barnacle give it a **"thatched" look**. This species can sometimes form column-like shapes under crowded conditions, which makes it more difficult to identify. The purple star (see p. 135) is the main predator and often limits the depth to which this barnacle is found. Females are known to brood their young over the winter months and release them when spring arrives. Individuals have been known to live for 15 years.

> GIANT BARNACLE
Balanus nubilis

Other name: Giant acorn barnacle.
Description: Outer shell is usually a dirty white. **Bright purple, yellow or red tissue near the beak-like central plates.** Large, flaring central opening (aperture).
Size: To 2³⁄4" (7 cm) in diameter, 4⁷⁄8" (12 cm) high.
Habitat: Normally subtidal, but on the exposed coast found in low intertidal zone to water 300' (91 m) deep.
Range: Southern Alaska to Monterey Bay, California.
Notes: The giant barnacle is sometimes observable while attached to pilings and rocks in the low intertidal zone. The feeding appendages reach out a full 2" (5 cm) or more with sweeping movements in an effort to feed. This action can sometimes be observed even while the barnacle is out of water. The barnacles' casings are sometimes found on beaches after being tossed on shore after winter storms. Coastal aboriginal people traditionally roasted giant barnacles in embers and ate them.

> ACORN BARNACLE
Balanus glandula

Other names: Common acorn barnacle; *Balanus glandulus*.
Description: White to gray, cone-shaped. Younger living specimens have visible dark black lining of cover plates; this is not easily seen in older individuals.
Size: To ³⁄4" (1.8 cm) in diameter, ³⁄8" (1 cm) high.
Habitat: On rocks in **high and mid-intertidal zones,** and on various hard-shelled animals in both exposed and protected sites.
Range: Aleutian Islands, Alaska to southern California.
Notes: The acorn barnacle can grow into elongated columns under crowded conditions, somewhat like the larger thatched barnacle (see p. 104). This barnacle produces between 2 and 6 broods per year, during the cooler months. Individuals have been known to live to 15 years. A similar species, the little brown barnacle (next page), is smaller with a brown coloration.

> LITTLE BROWN BARNACLE
Chthamalus dalli

Other names: Small acorn barnacle; buckshot barnacle.
Description: Grayish-brown shell. Relatively large central opening with a + pattern where cover plates meet.
Size: To 1/4" (6 mm) in diameter, 1/8" (4 mm) high.
Habitat: Normally attached to rock, **high intertidal zone**.
Range: Unalaska Island, Alaska to California.
Notes: The little brown barnacle is distinctive in that it does not crowd into spaces in such a way that produces elongated individuals. But under ideal conditions, it can reach populations of 60,300/yd² (72,000/m²). This species is known to grow higher on intertidal rocks than any other barnacles, so it must tolerate very long periods of time out of water in the hot sun. Some barnacles can lose up to 40 percent of the water in their bodies in less than 9 hours.

> SHELL BARNACLE
Solidobalanus hesperius

Other name: Formerly *Balanus hesperius*.
Description: Off-white in color, usually with pronounced ribs on lower portion of plates. Walls are solid, lacking internal tubes. Large opening.
Size: To 3/4" (2.1 cm) in diameter, 1/2" (1.4 cm) high.
Habitat: Normally on shells of living mollusks and crabs, in sites with muddy bottoms, in subtidal waters 60–215' (18–64 m) deep. Has also been found in intertidal holdfasts of some seaweeds.
Range: Alaska to Monterey, California.
Notes: This barnacle is commonly found on the shells of the Dungeness crab (see p. 121), Lewis's moonsnail (p. 72), various limpets and other mollusks.

> GOOSE BARNACLE
Pollicipes polymerus

Other names: Leaf barnacle; gooseneck barnacle; formerly *Mitella polymerus.*

Description: Cream-colored plates, generally dark brown body. Upper portion of body is supported by a flexible stalk (peduncle) which may grow to 6" (15 cm) in length. Individuals growing in the center of groups reach the greatest lengths.

Size: To 4" (10 cm) long.

Habitat: On exposed coast in areas subjected to strong wave action, mid-intertidal zone and lower.

Range: Sitka, Alaska to Baja California.

Notes: This barnacle is often found in close association with the California mussel (see p. 85). Their resilient stalks are tough enough to withstand the forces tossing them in the surf, and their presence indicates you are in an area subject to harsh ocean waves. Be ever watchful for an unexpected wave when you are in such areas. The goose barnacle is edible and has been exported from North America to Europe as a delicacy. Gulls, too, find this a tasty species and occasionally consume it in large numbers.

> PELAGIC GOOSE BARNACLE
Lepas anatifera

Other name: Common goose barnacle.

Description: Gray to bluish-gray plates, orange-brown to purplish-brown body with a brilliant scarlet-orange edge opening. An elongated stalk supports the flat, wedge-shaped body.

Size: To 6" (15 cm) long, 2³⁄₄" (7 cm) wide.

Habitat: Normally on driftwood, floating in the open ocean. Small individuals are sometimes found attached to seaweed, stranded on the beach.

Range: The oceans of the world.

Notes: This gregarious barnacle is a creature of the high seas. The young are attracted to floating objects which become home to hundreds or thousands of these barnacles. Once the

"colonies" have been afloat for some time, they mature and produce their young. To observe this species on shore, walk on the beach after a storm and look for a stranded float, bottle or log on which these barnacles have settled.

Shrimps, Crabs & Allies • Class Malacostraca

Members of the shrimp and crab clan have several similar characteristics, including an exterior skeleton, jointed legs, two pairs of antennae and many body segments.

A hard exterior skeleton is one of the characteristics of crabs, so as they grow they must shed their shells periodically. The new shells are soft and remain so for a few days while the crabs grow rapidly, hence the term "soft-shelled crab." Crabs are most vulnerable during this transition period.

Some shrimps are hermaphrodites—male when they are small, changing to female when they become adults. Females carry their eggs and protect them until they hatch. Shrimps, like crabs, are the focus of a large commercial fishery.

Isopods and Amphipods

>VOSNESENSKY'S ISOPOD
Idotea wosnesenskii

Other names: Olive green isopod; green isopod; rockweed isopod; kelp isopod.
Description: Brown, green or red with a broad, flat body and rounded tip on the abdomen.
Size: To 1³⁄₈" (3.5 cm) long.
Habitat: On various seaweeds or under rocks, high intertidal zone to water 53' (16 m) deep.
Range: Alaska to southern California.
Notes: Vosnesensky's isopod is very well adapted to living among seaweed and rocks. It is a master of disguise, usually cryptically colored and very difficult to find. Algae are the mainstay of its diet. This isopod was named in recognition of the work that the Russian zoologist Ilya Gavrilovich Vosnesensky conducted in Siberia, Alaska and California.

> CALIFORNIA BEACH HOPPER

Megalorchestia californiana

Other names: California beach flea; formerly *Orchestoidea californiana*.
Description: Ivory-white body, round and heavy. The **antennae are red in adults, orange in juveniles**, and longer than the body.
Size: The California beach hopper grows to 1¹/₈" (2.8 cm) long.
Habitat: At clean, fine sand beaches at the high tide mark and above.

This beach hopper and several other similar species are often found on the shore.

Range: BC to southern California.
Notes: Beach hoppers are sometimes called beach fleas, but this implies they are insects, which is not the case. This beach hopper is often found early in the morning, hiding among seaweed debris at the high tide mark once the tide recedes. At night, large numbers gather to feed on washed-up pieces of seaweed where the water laps onto the beach.

- - -

> SKELETON SHRIMP

Caprella sp.

Other name: Phantom shrimp.
Description: Green or brown elongated body with 4 leg-like appendages and grasping claws.
Size: To 2" (5.1 cm) long.
Habitat: On hydroids, eel-grass and seaweed near the low tide level and below in shallow water.
Range: BC to southern California.
Notes: The skeleton shrimp is not a shrimp at all, but an amphipod. Its shape approaches that of a shrimp. These fast-moving creatures feed upon tiny plants and animals. Females with obvious brood pouches can sometimes be found. The pouches are located on the third and fourth thoracic segments, as are the gills.

Shrimps

>SMOOTH BAY SHRIMP
Crangon stylirostris

Other name: Smooth crangon.
Description: Coloration of this shrimp closely resembles the sand in which it buries. Its carapace has no central spine.
Size: To 2³/₈" (6.1 cm) long.
Habitat: In exposed sandy areas, intertidal zone to water 264' (80 m) deep.
Range: Alaska to Santa Cruz, California.
Notes: This shrimp is capable of moving lightning-fast, which aids it greatly in avoiding predators. By carefully watching this species, you will notice that it prefers to bury itself in the sand whenever possible. To hide itself completely, it uses its long antennae to push sand over its body carefully, leaving only a tiny portion of its head uncovered. Tiny crustaceans and clams form the bulk of this species' diet.

>STOUT SHRIMP
Heptacarpus brevirostris

Other name: Short-spined shrimp.
Description: Colors range from brown to green in uniform colors or mottled with white, depending on surroundings. Body has a short nose-like blade (rostrum) and carapace is armed with 5 or 6 dorsal spines.
Size: To 2³/₈" (6.2 cm) long.
Habitat: On protected rocky beaches and in tidepools, mid-intertidal zone to water 420' (128 m) deep.
Range: Aleutian Islands, Alaska to San Francisco Bay, California.
Notes: The stout shrimp is one of the larger intertidal species and the most likely to be observed in tidepools if you watch carefully and wait patiently—these shrimp hide by day and may not move for extended periods of time. Stout shrimp are active by night when they come out to feed in tidepools. This species was harvested commercially in the San Francisco Bay area in the last century.

> Sitka Shrimp
Heptacarpus sitchensis

Other names: Sitka coastal shrimp; common coastal shrimp; formerly *Heptacarpus pictus*.
Description: Normally green with red diagonal stripes and blue dots. Stout body includes an elongated nose-like blade (rostrum).
Size: To 1" (2.8 cm) long.
Habitat: In gravel areas mixed with sand, and beneath rocks at low tide, mid-intertidal zone to 40' (12 m) deep.
Range: Alaska to Baja California.
Notes: On occasion transparent individuals can be found. They live in areas lacking in algae or eel-grass. Females have been seen carrying their eggs during May, June and September in BC.

> Blue Mud Shrimp
Upogebia pugettensis

Other names: Mud shrimp; marine crayfish.
Description: Gray to blue-gray, with 2 equal-sized claws.
Size: To 6" (15 cm) long, 1" (2.5 cm) high.
Habitat: In sand or mud flats, mid- to low intertidal zones.
Range: Southeast Alaska to Baja California.
Notes: A pair of blue mud shrimp live in a permanent U-shaped burrow. There they continually fan water through their burrow to obtain microscopic food. Hairs on the first two pairs of legs are used to strain this food from the water. In the fall these shrimp lay their yellow eggs, which develop slowly and hatch in the spring. The entrances to their burrows lack the distinctive volcano shape of the bay ghost shrimp's burrow (see below). The bay ghost shrimp is a similar species with a pink color overall and one greatly enlarged claw.

The blue mud shrimp's burrow partially excavated.

› BAY GHOST SHRIMP

Neotrypaea californiensis

Other names: Ghost shrimp; sand shrimp; California ghost shrimp; *Callianassa californiensis*.

Description: White with **pink, yellow or orange** highlights. **One claw is enlarged**, especially in the male.

Size: To 4" (10 cm) long.

Habitat: On sand or mud tide flats, mid- to low intertidal zones.

Range: Southeast Alaska to Baja California.

Notes: The bay ghost shrimp lives to 10 years in its J-shaped burrow. A characteristic volcano-shaped mound surrounds the burrow entrance. These non-permanent burrows may be as deep as 30" (75 cm). At least 9 different tenant species are known to live in the burrows while the owner is present. This shrimp lays its eggs in the spring and they hatch from June through August.

Male bay ghost shrimp.

Female with eggs.

Characteristic burrow mounds.

Crabs

› UMBRELLA CRAB

Cryptolithodes sitchensis

Other names: Turtle crab; butterfly crab.

Description: Color can include bright red, orange, gray or white. The flattened and flared carapace conceals crab's legs when viewed from above. Shell also includes a distinctive snout-like projection (rostrum).

Size: Carapace to 3½" (9 cm) wide.

Habitat: On bedrock and in tidepools of the outer coast in protected to semi-exposed sites, low intertidal zone to water 56' (17 m) deep.

Range: Torch Bay, Alaska to Point Loma, California.

Notes: This slow-moving crab is a great treat to find at the lowest of tides. It remains motionless, and its many color phases help it blend in well with its surroundings, so it often goes unnoticed. The umbrella crab feeds on a wide variety of organisms including calcareous red algae. Little else is known about the biology of this species.

>HAIRY CRAB
Hapalogaster mertensii

Other name: Tuft-haired crab.
Description: Brown to red in color. The fingers on the claws are often orange. Entire body is covered with bristles.
Size: Carapace to $1^3/8$" (3.5 cm) wide.
Habitat: In narrow crevices and on undersides of rocks stacked on top of other rocks, low intertidal zone to water 180' (55 m) deep.
Range: Aleutian Islands, Alaska to Puget Sound, Washington.
Notes: The hairy crab appears to have only 4 pairs of legs, and 4 pairs are apparently sufficient for all its normal activities, but a small fifth pair is hidden away beneath its abdomen. This crab is an omnivore, feeding on algae and small invertebrates. It is also capable of filter-feeding. A parasitic barnacle called the hairy-crab barnacle *Briarosaccus tenellus* has been found on the underside of this crab. This is truly a specialized barnacle—the hairy crab is its only known host.

>GRANULAR CLAW CRAB
Oedignathus inermis

Other names: Soft-bellied crab; papillose crab.
Description: Carapace is somewhat pear-shaped. The single large claw is covered in purple granular bumps.
Size: Carapace to 1" (2.5 cm) wide.
Habitat: In rock crevices and occasionally in mussel beds, mid-intertidal zone to water 50' (15 m) deep.
Range: Alaska to Pacific Grove, California.
Notes: This crab is well protected within crevices, its large claw often the only portion which is visible. A pair of these crabs often take up residence together in the same cavity. The granular claw crab uses its large clumsy but powerful claw to crush small mussels. The smaller left claw however is used effectively for grabbing, scraping and similar uses in feeding. The black oystercatcher *Haematopus bachmani* is known to prey upon this crab when it is found in mussel beds.

> FLATTOP CRAB

Petrolisthes eriomerus

Other names: Porcelain crab; flat-topped crab.

Description: Reddish brown to blue-gray with a flat, nearly circular shell and long whip-like antennae. **Blue spot at base of the movable part of the flat claws**, and **blue mouthparts**. Wrist segment (carpus) of claw is about 2 times longer than wide.

Size: Carapace to $^{3}/_{4}$" (1.9 cm) wide.

Habitat: Under rocks and among mussels in mussel beds, especially in areas with swift currents, low intertidal zone to water 284' (86 m) deep.

Range: Alaska to La Jolla, California.

Notes: Flattop crabs are also known to live together in groups of males, females and young. One dominant male does all or most of the breeding. The claws of this crab bear clusters of fine hairs which are used at night to gather food from rock surfaces. When a claw is dropped, it continues to pinch. Females often have two broods of young per year which range in number from 10 to 1,580 eggs per brood. This crab, like all porcelain crabs, has only 4 visible pairs of walking legs.

> FLAT PORCELAIN CRAB

Petrolisthes cinctipes

Other name: Smooth porcelain crab.

Description: Color varies from brown to blue. There is a **red spot at the base of the movable part of each claw**, and **red mouthparts**. Wrist segment (carpus) of claw is approximately $1^{1}/_{2}$ times longer than wide.

Size: Carapace to $^{7}/_{8}$" (2.4 cm) wide.

Habitat: Under rocks and in mussel beds, high and mid-intertidal zones.

Range: Queen Charlotte Islands, BC to Santa Barbara, California.

Notes: This crab is sometimes found in high numbers in beds of the California mussel (see p. 85). In some ideal locations, their numbers have been calculated to reach 719 individuals per square yard (860/m²). This crab, like all porcelain crabs, sheds its brittle claws or legs easily when it feels threatened. The missing appendages grow back after several molts.

>THICK-CLAWED PORCELAIN CRAB

Pachycheles rudis

Other name: Thickclaw porcelain crab.
Description: Dull brown with a rounded body and granule-covered claws. Claws large and unequal.
Size: Carapace to ³/₄" (1.8 cm) wide.
Habitat: Normally in pairs under rocks, in the empty burrows of rock-dwelling clams and similar sheltered locations, low intertidal zone to water 95' (29 m) deep.
Range: Kodiak, Alaska to Baja California.

The claws of all porcelain crabs are easily shed. This crab has shed one.

Notes: This crab uses its specialized mouthparts to filter out plankton and other microscopic food from the water. Unlike many types of crabs, male and female thick-clawed porcelain crabs grow to the same size.

>BERING HERMIT

Pagurus beringanus

Other name: *Eupagurus beringanus.*
Description: Bright scarlet spots and bands on light blue walking legs. Claws are also scarlet and covered in spines; right claw is much larger than left.
Size: Carapace to 1" (2.6 cm) long.
Habitat: In rocky areas, low intertidal zone to depths of 1,200' (364 m).
Range: Aleutian Islands, Alaska to Monterey, California.

Notes: The Bering hermit adds a splash of color to the low intertidal zone. It tends to use large, heavy shells, such as frilled dogwinkle (see p. 74) and dire whelk (p. 75), in which it can hide completely. During low tides this species is often attracted to shady rock crevices.

> GREENMARK HERMIT
Pagurus caurinus

Description: Antennae are red and unbanded. Legs have white bands, claws have orange tips.

Size: Carapace to 3/8" (1 cm) long.

Habitat: In both exposed and sheltered locations, low intertidal zone to water 413' (126 m) deep.

Range: Alaska to California.

Notes: This common hermit crab is often overlooked or thought to be the hairy hermit (see p. 117). The red antennae and absence of blue on the walking legs of the greenmark hermit crab help to confirm its identity.

> GRAINYHAND HERMIT
Pagurus granosimanus

Other name: Granular hermit crab.

Description: Dull green color, with blue or whitish spots or granules covering the body. Antennae are orange and unbanded.

Size: Carapace to 3/4" (1.9 cm) long.

Habitat: In rocky or gravel areas and tidepools, low intertidal zone to water 118' (36 m) deep.

Range: Alaska to Baja California.

Notes: This common species recycles larger, empty shells such as the black turban (see p. 67) and frilled dogwinkle (p. 74). The antics of this hermit crab, the clown of the seashore, can often be observed in tidepools. It reacts to the slightest movement by withdrawing into its shell, then falls from where it was and rolls to the bottom of its home, at which time it comes back out to do it all over again. This species is found lower intertidally than the hairy hermit crab (below).

>HAIRY HERMIT
Pagurus hirsutiusculus

Description: Noticeable narrow white band on lower portion of each walking leg, sometimes with a blue spot on upper portion of the same segment. Brownish antennae bear distinct bands. Much of the crab may be covered with hair.
Size: Carapace to ³⁄₄" (1.9 cm) long.
Habitat: In tidepools with sand or rock, in protected rocky areas, mid-intertidal zone to water as deep as 363' (110 m).
Range: Pribilof Islands, Alaska to southern California.
Notes: The hairy hermit chooses a variety of empty shells, including striped dogwinkle (see p. 75), purple olive (p. 77) and occasionally the turbans *Tegula* spp. (p. 67). This hermit often abandons its shell altogether after it has been picked up. This provides an excellent opportunity to see its entire body, normally hidden inside the shell.

>BLUEBAND HERMIT
Pagurus samuelis

Other name: Blue-handed hermit crab.
Description: Dull green, bright blue bands circle each of the walking legs near the tips. Young have white bands on walking legs. Antennae are bright red and unbanded.
Size: Carapace to ³⁄₄" (1.9 cm) long.
Habitat: In somewhat exposed locations near rocks, often in tidepools, high intertidal zone.
Range: Vancouver Island to Baja California.
Notes: The blueband hermit eats both plant and animal material. Most feeding activity occurs during the darkness of night. This hermit crab often uses the abandoned shells of the black turban (see p. 67) and striped dogwinkle (p. 75). Shells constantly change ownership in the world of hermit crabs. As they grow, they are ever watchful for new shells, even those currently being used by neighboring hermits.

>PACIFIC MOLE CRAB
Emerita analoga

Other name: Pacific sand crab.
Description: Tan to gray with an egg-shaped body that lacks claws.
Size: Carapace to 1³/8" (3.5 cm) long.
Habitat: This surf-loving crab moves up and down the beach with the tides.
Range: Oregon to Chile, with a few records as far north as Kodiak, Alaska.

This crab is usually found buried in the sand.

Notes: This crab burrows into the sand backwards so that only its head and antennae remain at the surface. Its long, feathery antennae are used to catch plankton and detritus, its prime food. If disturbed, these crabs disappear into the sand in mere seconds—truly amazing to watch. Temporary populations have been found north of Oregon. These begin with larvae reaching new sites via ocean currents, then individuals successfully grow to maturity. These are unable to reproduce, however, and the colony eventually disappears.

>GRACEFUL DECORATOR CRAB
Oregonia gracilis

Other name: Decorator crab.
Description: Carapace is drab and often too well camouflaged to be visible. Triangular shell is pointed at the front, wide and rounded at the back. A pair of long horns elongate the "snout area." Legs are noticeably elongated.
Size: Carapace to 1¹/2" (3.9 cm) wide.
Habitat: Among seaweed, intertidal zone to water 1,439' (436 m) deep.
Range: Bering Sea to Monterey Bay, California.
Notes: This species is known for its elaborate camouflage which is made of seaweeds, hydroids, sponges, bryozoans and virtually anything available. These it carefully fastens on its upper shell or carapace and legs with small, curved setae (velcro-like hooks).

>Shield-backed Kelp Crab
Pugettia producta

Other names: Kelp crab; northern kelp crab.
Description: Generally olive in color, with varying amounts of red or yellow in adults. Distinctive smooth, **shield-shaped carapace.**
Size: Carapace to 3⅝" (9.3 cm) wide.
Habitat: Usually in or on seaweed, especially bull kelp (see p. 165), intertidal zone to water 240' (73 m) deep.
Range: Alaska to Baja California.
Notes: The shield-backed kelp crab feeds primarily on kelp or large brown seaweed, but will feed on a variety of organisms if kelp is not available. The smooth carapace closely matches the algae it is often found upon. In the fall, adults migrate to kelp in deeper water. Here they congregate to feed and mate until December, when they return to shallower waters. Occasionally barnacles grow on the backs of adults, but this species does not camouflage itself as other related species do. Be sure to check pilings while at the dock. Large adults can often be found there.

• •

>Graceful Kelp Crab
Pugettia gracilis

Other names: Kelp crab; graceful rock crab; slender crab.
Description: Highly variable color, ranging from white to bright red, often ornamented with small amounts of seaweed, sponges or bryozoa. Fingers of claws blue or gray, tipped with orange.
Size: Carapace to 1½" (4 cm) wide.
Habitat: Among rocks and algae, from low intertidal zone to water 460' (140 m) deep. Young individuals are often found among eel-grass.
Range: Aleutian Islands, Alaska to Monterey, California.
Notes: The first noticeable feature is the decorations attached to this crab's shell. This species, like all crabs, attach and keep their eggs on the female until the young are ready to hatch. The eggs are attached in such a way that oxygen can reach each egg while water circulates.

• •

> HELMET CRAB
Telmessus cheiragonus

Other name: Horse crab.
Description: Yellowish-brown sometimes with red or orange added as well. Characteristic tiny hairs cover all surfaces.
Size: Carapace to 3¼" (8.3 cm) long, 4" (9.7 cm) wide.
Habitat: Intertidal zone to 360' (110 m) deep.
Range: Bering Sea to California.
Notes: During the early spring, this crab is often observed intertidally during the breeding season, typically in areas with an abundance of seaweed in which the crab can hide. This species is known to feed on eel-grass, algae, snails, bivalves and worms.

> RED ROCK CRAB
Cancer productus

Other names: Red crab; red cancer crab.
Description: Brick red in color. Shell has smooth, saw-like outline on front, and 5 equal rounded "scallops" between the eyes. **Tips of claws are black**.
Size: Carapace to 7" (18 cm) wide.
Habitat: Lower intertidal zone to water 260' (79 m) deep.
Range: Alaska to Baja California.
Notes: The red rock crab, like all of the *Cancer* clan, is a carnivore. Its heavy claws are strong enough to crack open the shells of barnacles and snails. It is an opportunist, feeding also on small living crabs and dead fish. The young of this native species are often found in the intertidal zone. Their coloration ranges from stripes of various colors to near-white, but the shape of this crab does not change. The **outline of its carapace resembles the letter D**. The red rock crab is popular in the sport fishery.

The defensive posture.

Juvenile crab.

Juvenile crab.

>PYGMY ROCK CRAB
Cancer oregonensis

Other names: Hairy cancer crab; Oregon cancer crab; Oregon rock crab.

Description: Dark red, with **round carapace** and hairy legs. **Claws are tipped with black.**

Size: Carapace **to 1³⁄4" (4.7 cm) wide**.

Habitat: Under rocks, low intertidal zone to 1,435' (435 m) deep.

Range: Pribilof Islands, Alaska to Los Angeles, California.

Notes: Mating takes place in the spring after the females molt. Courtship behaviour includes males carrying females prior to their molting and continuing to carry them, after mating, until their new shells have hardened. Females store the sperm until late fall or winter and spawn in February, carrying as many as 33,000 eggs. Barnacles are the primary food for the pygmy rock crab.

>DUNGENESS CRAB
Cancer magister

Other names: Edible cancer crab; commercial crab; Pacific crab.

Description: Red-brown to **purple shell** with spine-tipped edge on front half. Shell widest at the tenth tooth. **Claws with white tips.**

Size: Carapace **to 9" (22.5 cm) wide**.

Habitat: On sandy bottoms, low intertidal zone to water 759' (230 m) deep.

Range: Alaska to Santa Barbara, California.

Notes: The Dungeness crab is harvested both commercially and recreationally. Females lay up to 2.5 million eggs and this species is known to live at least 6 years. It is an active carnivore, which feeds on at least 40 different species including shrimp, small clams, oysters, worms and fish. Dungeness crabs spend a great deal of time buried under the sand. In the spring, they can often be found in the low intertidal zone buried in sandy tidepools. This is where they hide while waiting for their new shells to harden.

Young burying itself in the sand.

Underside of male.

Underside of female.

> BLACK-CLAWED CRAB

Lophopanopeus bellus

Description: Carapace varies in color from orange to purple or white. A total of 3 spines project forward on the sides of the carapace, **claw fingers usually dark**.

Size: Carapace to 1¹/2" (4 cm) wide.

Habitat: In sand or gravel, low intertidal zone to water 264' (80 m).

Range: Alaska to Point Sur, California.

Notes: The black-clawed crab eats a variety of food including various algae, mussels and barnacles. Females are known to have two broods of young each year, each containing 6,000 to 36,000 eggs.

> STRIPED SHORE CRAB

Pachygrapsus crassipes

Description: Most often green, but may be red or purple with **black stripes across front**.

Size: Carapace to 1³/4" (4.7 cm) wide.

Habitat: In tidepools, high and mid-intertidal zones.

Range: Oregon to Gulf of California.

Notes: This crab is often found in tidepools. Well adapted to be out of the water, it comes out in large numbers to feed, especially among eel-grass. Its primary food is algae, which it picks up and brings to its mouth with alternating claws, seemingly shovelling it in with salad forks! There is also a report of this lively species capturing flies at low tide. Its main predators are gulls and raccoons. Striped shore crabs engage in interesting courtship behaviour. The female releases a chemical (pheromone) to attract males. Then a sort of dance begins where a male turns over onto his back and the female walks over him. Approximately 50,000 eggs are eventually produced by the female, once or twice each year. This crab, a native of North America, is often said to have been introduced from Asia, but in fact it was introduced to Asia in the late 1800s.

>YELLOW SHORE CRAB

Hemigrapsus oregonensis

Other name: Green shore crab, hairy shore crab.
Description: Usually green or grayish-green in color, but often white or mottled when young. **Fine hairs grow on the legs.**
Size: Carapace to 1⅞" (4.9 cm) wide.
Habitat: In sheltered areas under rocks and among eel-grass (see p. 183) in sandy areas, high to low intertidal zones.
Range: Alaska to Baja California.

Notes: This crab is primarily a herbivore, feeding on green algae such as sea lettuce (see p. 157). But it also is a scavenger of small organisms and may even filter-feed, separating food particles from the water with special parts of its mouth. An orange-red nemertean (ribbon worm) is a known predator of the eggs of this species and occasionally the purple shore crab (below). The purple shore crab is a similar species, but has red-purple spots on its claws.

>PURPLE SHORE CRAB

Hemigrapsus nudus

Other name: Purple rock crab.
Description: Color varies from purple to red-brown, with **red-purple spots usually present** on the claws. **No hair,** spines or other coverings on shell or legs (hence its name, *nudus*)—a useful feature to help with identification.
Size: Carapace to 2" (5.6 cm) wide.

Habitat: Under rocks and among seaweed, mid- and low intertidal zones. Often found out of the water on the shore.
Range: Alaska to Turtle Bay, Mexico.
Notes: The purple shore crab feeds mainly at night, consuming green algae such as sea lettuce (see p. 157). When this crab is discovered under a rock, it often walks sideways in an effort to escape and find a new hiding spot. Predators of adult crabs include the glaucous-winged gull *Larus glaucescens* and white-winged scoter *Melanitta fusca.*

>GAPER PEA CRAB
Pinnixa littoralis

Other name: Pea crab.
Description: White with dark markings. Dark markings are especially visible in the male.
Size: Carapace to 1" (2.7 cm) wide.
Habitat: In mantle cavity of primarily the fat gaper (see p. 91), low intertidal zone to subtidal water 300' (91 m) deep.
Range: Prince William Sound, Alaska to Baja California.

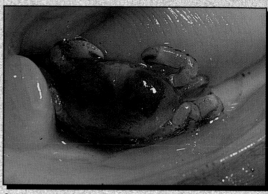

Gaper pea crab in fat gaper *Tresus capax.*

Notes: Gaper pea crabs live in pairs, inside the cavity of a clam in such a way that they do not harm the host. The female is much larger than the male. The young are sometimes found in the cavities of many species of clams as well as in larger limpets. Adults are most often found in the fat gaper, and occasionally Nuttall's cockle (see p. 91), the Pacific gaper (p. 92) and others.

Fat gaper *Tresus capax.*

Arachnids • Class Arachnida

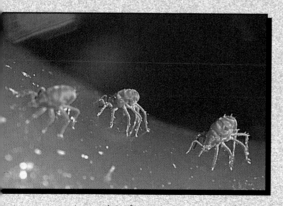

>RED VELVET MITE
Neomolgus littoralis

Other name: Intertidal mite.
Description: Bright scarlet red. Short dense hairs cover this mite, but cannot be seen without a microscope.
Size: To 1/8" (3 mm) long.
Habitat: High intertidal zone.
Range: Alaska to California.
Notes: The red velvet mite is related to spiders and ticks, which have 8 legs rather than 6, as found on insects. It is often seen scurrying about the high intertidal zone, in the heat of the day. This species has been observed using its snout-like mouthparts to feed on the fluids of dead flies. Additional studies are needed to determine other foods and the general natural history of this brightly colored arachnid.

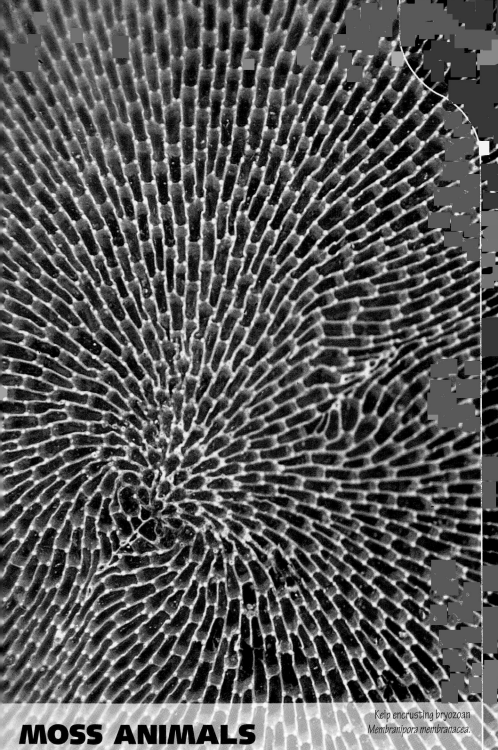

Kelp encrusting bryozoan
Membranipora membranacea.

MOSS ANIMALS
Phylum Bryozoa

Moss animals or bryozoans are an often misidentified group of nearly 2,000 different species. They live hanging from marine algae, encrusting on rocks and shells, or growing upright from a rock crevice. A bryozoan colony comprises thousands of individuals. The colony reproduces and grows by budding. Some species are rigid, others are flexible and sway in the water, still others are gelatinous. The bryozoan has a primitive nerve system but lacks a heart and vascular system.

▷ FLUTED BRYOZOAN

Hippodiplosia insculpta

Description: Yellow-brown to orange with double-fluted fronds.
Size: Colonies to 5" (12.5 cm) or more in diameter.
Habitat: Attached to rocks, mid-intertidal to subtidal water 772' (234 m) deep.
Range: Gulf of Alaska to Gulf of California and Costa Rica.
Notes: Touching this bryozoan reveals the hard nature of the species. It has been noted that in northern colonies, where the water is much cooler, larger individuals (zooids) may be found.

>SEA-LICHEN BRYOZOAN
Dendrobeania lichenoides

Other name: Sea mat bryozoan.
Description: Tan or brown with numerous petal-like, irregularly shaped fronds.
Size: Fronds to 1" (2.5 cm) in diameter.
Habitat: In shaded, protected, rocky areas, low intertidal zone to subtidal waters 300' (90 m) deep.
Range: Alaska to southern California.
Notes: This species attaches to a wide variety of substrates including shells, rocks and worm tubes. Countless numbers of microscopic tentacles cover bryozoans. These tentacles are used to filter-feed on phytoplankton, bacteria and detritus. This food is then moved to the central mouth of each individual by tiny hairs on the tentacles.

>KELP ENCRUSTING BRYOZOAN
Membranipora membranacea

Other names: Encrusting bryozoan; lacy-crust bryozoan; kelp lace.
Description: White in color, forming thin, flat colonies with small, rectangular cell-like structures. Individuals tend to crowd together, radiating from the center.
Size: Colony to more than 3" (7.6 cm) in diameter.
Habitat: On kelp fronds, floats and rocks.
Range: Alaska to Baja California, and all temperate regions of the world.
Notes: The kelp encrusting bryozoan is most often found in the spring through fall. It is commonly found on several species of kelp or brown algae including bull kelp (see p. 165). This beautifully patterned species starts growing from the center and radiates outward from the oldest portion. The cryptic nudibranch (p. 78) is sometimes found living on this bryozoan, but careful inspection is required to see it.

> ROSY BRYOZOAN

Eurystomella bilabiata

Description: Rose-red to orange-red with a distinctive hat-shaped opening for each individual.
Size: Colony to 2" (5 cm) in diameter.
Habitat: On stones or shells, low intertidal zone to subtidal waters 211' (64 m) deep.
Range: Alaska to central California.
Notes: This is an encrusting species in which many individuals (zooids) live side by side on a substrate. Each is enclosed in a case adjacent to its neighbors'. The colony expands when individuals bud off, producing new animals.

> BRANCHED-SPINE BRYOZOAN

Flustrellidra corniculata

Other name: *Flustrella cervicornis*
Description: Tan to brown with numerous spines covering the colony, giving it a fuzzy appearance.
Size: Colony to 4" (10 cm) long.
Habitat: Often found on various seaweeds, low intertidal zone to subtidal waters 248' (75 m) deep.
Range: Alaska to California.
Notes: The distinctive branched-spine bryozoan is a cold water species, also found in northern Europe. It looks somewhat like a fuzzy seaweed and has a soft, leather-like texture.

Purple star
Pisaster ochraceus.

SPINY-SKINNED ANIMALS
Phylum Echinodermata

The echinoderms (spiny-skinned) are a large group of animals. All members of this group have calcareous plates covered with a soft layer of skin. The size of the plates varies from large and conspicuous, as in most species (e.g. sea urchins), to inconspicuous (e.g. sea cucumbers). Locally the echinoderms consist of sea stars, brittle stars, sea urchins, sand dollars and sea cucumbers.

Sea Stars • Class Asteroidea

Sea stars were once referred to as starfish, but sea star is a much better name as no individuals in this group swim, have scales or are edible. Sea stars feed on a wide variety of foods. Some of the more active species can actually capture live snails or other stars, while some slower species feed on various seaweeds. Movement is made possible by many small tube feet on the underside of each ray.

Animals in this class have truly remarkable powers of regeneration. Entire limbs can be regenerated and in some species, whole sea stars can be regenerated from a single ray with a portion of the central disc or body.

> BAT STAR

Asterina miniata

Other names: Broad-disc sea star; sea bat; webbed sea star; formerly *Patiria miniata*.
Description: Has been observed in nearly every color of the rainbow. Normally 5 webbed arms, but sometimes 4–9 arms.
Size: To 6" (15 cm) in diameter.
Habitat: Normally on exposed sites with rock bottoms covered in surf-grass, algae, sponges and bryozoans, low intertidal zone to water 960' (293 m) deep.
Range: Sitka, Alaska to Baja California.

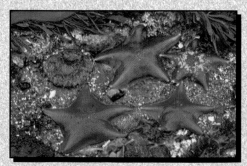

Notes: The bat star has been kept in captivity for more than 16 years and is thought to live up to 30 years. It is an omnivore, feeding on plants and animals both dead and alive. The bat star worm *Ophiodromus pugettensis*, a segmented worm, is often found living commensally on the underside of this sea star.

>LEATHER STAR
Dermasterias imbricata

Other name: Garlic star.
Description: Mottled red-brown to orange. 5 rays. A slippery secretion covers the surface.
Size: To 10" (25 cm) in diameter.
Habitat: On rocky shores, low intertidal zone to water 300' (91 m) deep.
Range: Prince William Sound, Alaska to southern California.
Notes: Tidepoolers can easily recognize this common species. The leather star feels like wet leather and often smells like garlic or sulphur. Its diet includes the giant green anemone (see p. 36), proliferating

The leather star is known for its slippery surface.

anemone (p. 37), red-beaded anemone (p. 38), purple sea urchin (p. 138) and several other invertebrates which it swallows whole and digests internally.

Underwater, in a tidepool.

>MORNING SUN STAR
Solaster dawsoni

Other name: Dawson's sun star.
Description: Color varies from gray to yellow, brown or red. Normally 11–13 arms, occasionally 8–10 or 14–15 arms.
Size: To 12" (30 cm) across.
Habitat: On mud, sand, gravel or rock, low intertidal zone to water 1,386' (420 m) deep.
Range: Alaska to Monterey Bay, California.
Notes: This sea star, one of more than 2,000 species of stars found throughout the world, specializes in feeding on other sea stars. Included in its menu are the striped sun star (see below), mottled star (p. 133), leather star (above), Pacific blood star (p. 132) and occasionally even its own species. It has also been known to feed on the stiff-footed sea cucumber (see p. 142).

› STRIPED SUN STAR

Solaster stimpsoni

Other names: Sun star; Stimpson's sun star.
Description: Blue, pink, red or orange with a **blue or purple stripe down each slender arm**. Usually 10 arms, occasionally only 9.
Size: To 16" (40 cm) across.
Habitat: In rocky areas, very low intertidal zone to subtidal waters 2,013' (610 m) deep.
Range: Bering Sea to Salt Point, California.
Notes: The striped sun star feeds on a variety of invertebrates, including sea cucumbers, lampshells and tunicates. This species is occasionally found in the intertidal zone. Its chief enemy is the morning sun star (see above).

› PACIFIC BLOOD STAR

Henricia leviuscula

Other names: Blood star; Pacific henricia.
Description: Color varies widely from blood red to tan, yellow, orange and purple. Typically 5 slender arms, occasionally 4–6.
Size: To 8" (20 cm) in diameter.
Habitat: On or under rocks covered with growth (sponges, etc.), in protected areas from low-tide mark to water 1,425' (435 m) deep.
Range: Aleutian Islands, Alaska to Baja California.
Notes: This common star feeds primarily upon sponges. Small females brood their bright red-orange eggs in darkness from January through March. Larger individuals do not brood their eggs at all, but release them directly into deeper water. The vivid color of this sea star is often the reason beachcombers take it home, but its color fades when it dries. Rather than removing it from its habitat, try taking a photograph or making a sketch.

Some individuals are tan in color.

>MOTTLED STAR
Evasterias troschelii

Other name: Troschel's sea star.
Description: Orange, brown or blue-gray with or without mottling. Small central disc with **5 long, slender arms**.
Size: To 16" (40 cm) in diameter, but most individuals are much smaller.
Habitat: In protected areas, on rock or sand bottoms, low intertidal zone to water 230' (70 m) deep.
Range: Prince William Sound, Alaska to central California.
Notes: The colors of the mottled star are often drab in com-

parison to many of the other stars found in this region. This species is found in sheltered areas—a useful identifying feature when distinguishing this star from the similar purple star (p. 135), which often makes its home in areas with heavy surf. The mottled star feeds on a wide variety of invertebrates, including bivalves, limpets, barnacles, snails, tunicates and brachiopods.

>SIX-RAYED STAR
Leptasterias hexactis

Other names: Broad six-rayed sea star; six-armed sea star.
Description: Color varies from green to black, brown, orange, yellow or red, often with a pattern. Normally has 6 rays.
Size: To 4" (10 cm) in diameter.
Habitat: On rocky shores, high intertidal to subtidal zones and below. Frequently found under rocks in intertidal areas.
Range: BC to southern California.
Notes: This small star is often found tightly attached to the underside of a rock. It feeds on sea cucumbers, barnacles, chitons, mussels, limpets and snails. Most feeding occurs during the summer months; little if any food is eaten over the winter months. The female broods her egg mass under her disc for 6–8 weeks before the eggs hatch. This star reaches maturity at approximately 2 years.

› PAINTED SEA STAR
Orthasterias koehleri

Other names: Rainbow sea star; long-armed sea star; long-rayed sea star.
Description: Color varies from vivid rosy pink to red with gray or yellow banding. Prominent sharp spines grace the dorsal surface.
Size: To 16" (42 cm) in diameter.
Habitat: Very low intertidal zone to water 825' (250 m) deep.
Range: Alaska to the Channel Islands, California.
Notes: This beautiful sea star is a carnivore, feeding on small snails, limpets, clams, scallops, barnacles, tunicates and other similar invertebrates. Like several other stars, this species actually pushes its stomach between the shells of a clam to begin digesting its meal.

› GIANT PINK STAR
Pisaster brevispinus

Other name: Short-spined sea star.
Description: Characteristically pink to almost white. Short spines cover the dorsal side.
Size: To 26" (64 cm) in diameter.
Habitat: Sand or mud bottoms are the normal habitat for this large sea star found from the low intertidal zone to water 330' (100 m) deep.
Range: Vancouver Island to Monterey Bay, California.
Notes: This large sea star feeds on the Pacific geoduck (see p. 99), giant barnacle (p. 105) and eccentric sand dollar (p. 139), among other species. The size of the individual sea star determines the size of its prey. This species is very similar to the purple star (below), which is a smaller size and a purple or ochre color.

> PURPLE STAR
Pisaster ochraceus

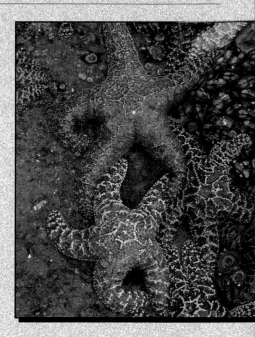

Other names: Ochre star; common sea star.
Description: Has 3 color phases: **purple, brown and yellow**. Normally **5 stout arms**, but occasionally 4–7. A loose network of white calcareous plates stiffens the body.
Size: To 14" (35 cm) in diameter.
Habitat: Along **exposed** and protected rocky shorelines, mid- to lower intertidal zones to water 300' (90 m) deep.
Range: Alaska to Baja California.
Notes: This is the most common sea star found in our intertidal zones. It feeds on mussels, abalone, chitons, barnacles and snails. Many prey species can detect this star when it is nearby and are able to escape. But its favorite prey species, including the California mussel (see p. 85) and the goose barnacle (p. 107), are attached and are unable to escape.

> SUNFLOWER STAR
Pycnopodia helianthoides

Other name: Twenty-rayed sea star.
Description: Yellow, orange, brown, pink, red or purple. Typically 24 arms and a broad disc covered with a soft skin.
Size: Normally to 39" (1 m) in diameter; occasionally even larger.
Habitat: On soft bottoms and rocky shores, low intertidal zone to water 1,440' (437 m) deep.
Range: Prince William Sound, Alaska to southern California.

Notes: A good-sized sunflower star has an estimated 15,000 tube feet on its body. It is the largest and fastest sea star found in the Pacific Northwest and is a voracious feeder, preying on many large clams and crustaceans. It has also been observed to feed on dead squid. It engulfs the indigestible squid pen, which is too large to pass normally from the star and which is extruded through the soft upper part of the star's body. The Alaska king crab *Paralithodes camtschaticus* has been observed feeding on the sunflower star.

Brittle Stars • Class Ophiuroidea

Most brittle stars shun light and during daylight hours are normally found hiding under rocks or in similar situations. Most species live in the tropics, but a few species inhabit the Pacific Northwest. When stressed, these delicate creatures often shed their arms, then regenerate new ones in time.

› DAISY BRITTLE STAR

Ophiopholis aculeata

Other names: Serpent star; painted brittlestar.

Description: Wide range of colors and patterns. **Central disc is a scalloped shape with bulges between the arms.**

Size: Disc to $9/10"$ (2.2 cm) in diameter. **Length of arms to 3.5–4 times diameter of disc.**

Habitat: Under stones, in algal holdfasts and rocky shores, low intertidal zone to water 5,465' (1,657 m) deep.

Range: Bering Sea to southern California.

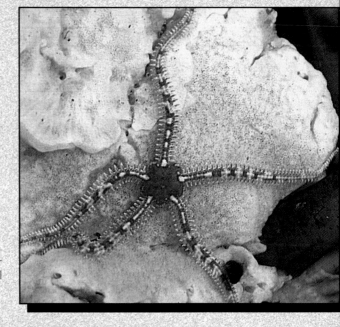

Notes: This common species, whose name comes from the flower-like shape of its disc, is more abundant in the northern part of its range. Like other brittle stars, it feeds by scraping minute organisms from rock with its specialized tube feet. The food then enters the stomach, which takes up most of the body cavity. Unlike the sea star, the brittle star cannot extrude its stomach to feed. Strangely enough, there is no intestine or anus; instead food is absorbed along the alimentary canal and wastes go back out the mouth.

> Dwarf Brittle Star
Amphipholis squamata

Other names: Small brittle star; serpent star; holdfast brittle star; brooding brittle star; *Axiognathus squamatus*.
Description: Gray, tan or orange. A white spot is found near the base of each arm on the **round disc, which lacks bulges.**
Size: Disc to 1/10" (5 mm) in diameter. **Length of arms to 3–4 times diameter of disc.**
Habitat: Among rock, sand and loose gravel, high intertidal zone to water 2,730' (828 m) deep.
Range: Alaska to southern California.
Notes: This small brittle star is very mobile and can often be found in tidepools. It broods its young. Its diet consists primarily of diatoms and detritus. It is capable of producing bioluminescence. Cells at the base of the spines can be stimulated chemically in the laboratory setting to emit a glowing yellow-green luminescence. The significance of this is unknown at present.

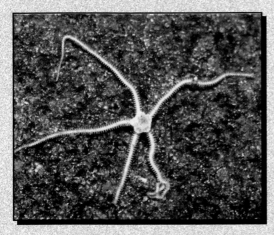

> Black And White Brittle Star
Amphipholis pugetana

Other name: Puget dwarf brittle star.
Description: Banded with white and gray, or all white to grayish.
Size: Disc to 1/2" (1 cm) in diameter. **Length of arms to 8–10 times diameter of disc.**
Habitat: In tidepools and under rocks, high intertidal zone to subtidal waters.
Range: Alaska to southern California.
Notes: This fast-moving species is often found in large numbers, which probably enhances its chances for survival. It is often found higher on the beach than other brittle stars. Its arms do not fall off as easily as those of other species. Diatoms and a variety of decaying matter are its main food sources. This star does not brood its young.

Sea Urchins & Sand Dollars • Class Echinoidea
There are over 800 different species of sea urchins and sand dollars worldwide. These animals feed with the help of a unique jaw-like apparatus known as Aristotle's lantern, an arrangement of parts, including teeth, that makes it possible to eat tough seaweeds.

Sea urchins are covered with movable spines, which come in a wide range of colors and which can be blunt or sharp, long or short. Urchins make their way into our kitchens on occasion: their roe (see red sea urchin, p. 139) are eaten raw in sushi, they are sautéed or added to omelettes or soups, and they are cooked in a variety of other ways.

> GREEN SEA URCHIN

Strongylocentrotus droebachiensis

Description: Usually **green-brown**. Length of **short spines** is normally less than a third the diameter of the round skeleton (test).
Size: Test to 3¼" (8.3 cm) wide, spines to 1" (2.5 cm).
Habitat: In both sheltered and exposed kelp beds and rocky areas, low intertidal zone to water 427' (130 m) deep with reports to 3,937' (1,200 m) in the Atlantic.
Range: Alaska to Puget Sound, Washington.
Notes: In some areas green sea urchins have become so numerous that it is difficult to walk without treading on them. This species is also found on our Atlantic coast and in Europe. The young of a similar species, the purple sea urchin (see below) can also be greenish in color but with stout spines.

> PURPLE SEA URCHIN

Strongylocentrotus purpuratus

Other name: Purple spined sea urchin.
Description: **Purple** or purplish-green, spherical and **covered with short, stout spines**. Length of these spines is approximately a third the diameter of the round skeleton (test).
Size: Test to 4" (10 cm) wide, spines to 1" (2.5 cm) long.
Habitat: On exposed rocky shorelines, low intertidal zone to water 525' (160 m) deep.
Range: BC to Baja California.
Notes: This species is often found in large groups in the lower intertidal zone. Its chief food is seaweed. Some individuals have been found to live longer than 30 years. It is estimated that one female urchin can produce up to 20 million eggs in one year. Purple sea urchins are capable of excavating holes in rock, by using their sharp spines and teeth over time. While residing inside their holes, urchins are protected from the pounding surf.

>RED SEA URCHIN
Strongylocentrotus franciscanus

Other name: Giant red urchin.
Description: Red to purple skeleton (test) with **elongated spines**, similarly colored. Length of spines is normally half the diameter of the test.
Size: Test to 6½" (17 cm) wide, spines to 3" (7.6 cm) long.
Habitat: On exposed rocky shorelines, low intertidal zone to water 300' (91 m) deep.
Range: Alaska to Baja California.
Notes: This urchin is not as common intertidally as the purple sea urchin but can often be found in the same areas. The red urchin feeds on

Typical red sea urchin.

pieces of brown and red seaweed. Adults have been known to reach 20 years of age. The reproductive organs (roe) of the red sea urchin are harvested for shipment to Japan. This delicacy is eaten raw as a garnish for sushi and numerous other dishes. The purple sea urchin (see above) is a similar species, easily distinguished by its short spines.

Red sea urchin with purple coloration.

>ECCENTRIC SAND DOLLAR
Dendraster excentricus

Other name: Pacific sand dollar.
Description: Covering of tiny spines and tube feet give live specimens a very dark, velvety, purple color; dead shells (tests) are off-white. 5-leafed pattern of tiny holes on dorsal side of test.
Size: To 3" (7.6 cm) in diameter.
Habitat: On sandy beaches, low intertidal zone to water 50' (15 m) deep.
Range: Alaska to Baja California.
Notes: In subtidal areas, density of sand dollars can be staggering—more than 523 per square yard (625/m²), a great deal more than are found intertidally. Sand dollars are unable to right themselves if upturned, and eventually die. Individuals living in intertidal areas are known to bury themselves, while those in quiet subtidal areas do not. In exposed subtidal areas, sand dollars lie flat, while in protected subtidal areas they rest at an angle to the waves. The sand dollar eats by moving diatoms and detritus to its central mouth with its tiny hair-like cilia. Individuals have been known to live 13 years.

The test (shell).

Sea Cucumbers • Class Holothuroidea

Sea cucumbers are echinoderms (spiny-skinned animals) which are related to sea urchins. Most species have separate sexes. Reproduction occurs in two ways: some species produce many small eggs which eventually develop into pelagic larvae; other species produce a few rather large yolk-filled eggs which hatch directly into small cucumbers.

> CALIFORNIA SEA CUCUMBER
Parastichopus californicus

Other names: Giant sea cucumber; large red cucumber; common sea cucumber; California stichopus; formerly *Stichopus californicus*.

Description: Usually mottled reddish-brown with soft projections along the entire body. Body is elongated and filled with water.

Size: To nearly 20" (50 cm) long, to 3" (7.6 cm) in diameter.

Habitat: In exposed and sheltered areas, low intertidal zone to water 295' (90 m) deep.

Young in tidepool

Range: Gulf of Alaska to Baja California.

Notes: The separate sexes of this sea cucumber mature at 4 years. The animal is harvested for the thin muscles running along the inside of the body wall. Its chief predator other than man is the sunflower star (see p. 135), to which it has been known to react in an interesting manner when in extreme danger. The internal organs are ejected out the anus, producing a sticky pile of viscera which could distract a predator. These organs are regenerated within 6–8 weeks.

>Orange Sea Cucumber

Cucumaria miniata

Other names: Red sea gherkin; red sea cucumber.

Description: Red with elongated shape, smooth skin and tentacles at one end of the body.

Size: To 4–8" (10–20 cm) long.

Habitat: In cobble and rocky areas, low intertidal zone to 330' (100 m) deep.

Range: Alaska to central California.

Notes: The striped sun star (see p. 132) is an enemy from which this sea cucumber tries to flee by producing a number of violent contractions in rapid succession. Scientists have found that the blood of this common species is very similar to that of trout and other fish.

Orange sea cucumber with expanded feeding tentacles.

❯ STIFF-FOOTED SEA CUCUMBER
Eupentacta quinquesemita

Other names: White sea gherkin; white sea cucumber.
Description: White to cream-colored; shaped some-what like a sausage with **rigid, spiny-looking tube feet.** 8 large branched tentacles and 2 small-sized tentacles are located at one end of the body.
Size: To 3" (10 cm) long.

Habitat: In crevices or between rocks, low intertidal zone to shallow subtidal waters.
Range: Sitka, Alaska to Baja California.
Notes: The enemies of this sea cucumber include the morning sun star (see p. 131), striped sun star (p. 132) and sunflower star (p. 135). The six-rayed star (p. 133) feeds on juvenile stiff-footed sea cucumber.

A creeping pedal sea cucumber out of water.

❯ CREEPING PEDAL SEA CUCUMBER
Psolus chitonoides

Other names: Slipper sea cucumber; armored sea cucumber.
Description: Bright red to pale yellow, red tentacles with white tips. Flat body is covered with several calcareous plates.
Size: To 5" (12.5 cm) in diameter.
Habitat: On rocks in exposed and sheltered inlets, low inter-tidal zone to subtidal water 815' (247 m) deep.
Range: Pribilof Islands to Baja California.
Notes: Out of the water, this cucumber resembles a chiton. In the water, however, its feeding tentacles are extended and become visible. Each tentacle holds a sticky pad which is used to catch tiny food particles from the water. The tentacles are then inserted in the mouth to be cleaned off. Various sea stars and the red rock crab (see p. 120) feed on this sea cucumber and some fish nibble on its tentacles, even though it produces various toxic chemicals to deter predators.

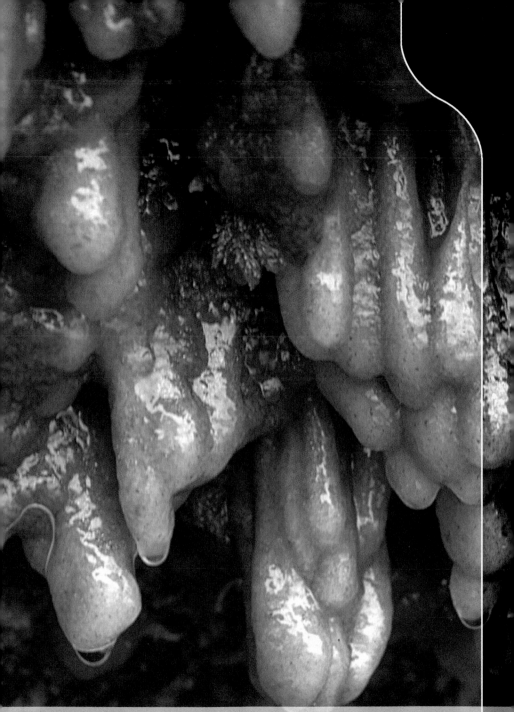

Unknown species of tunicate.

TUNICATES
Phylum Urochordata

Sea Squirts • Class Ascidiacea

There are three types of sea squirts, or tunicates: solitary, colonial and compound. All are covered with an exterior coating called a tunic, hence the name tunicate. Solitary species are oval, elongated or irregular in shape, and an individual is usually attached directly to the substrate by its side or a base. All sea squirts have 2 siphons, one to obtain water for food and for respiration, and the other to expel water and non-food particles. Colonial or social tunicates reproduce by budding or cloning to produce additional individuals from a single original member. Compound sea squirts are much different: many individuals (zooids) are packed together and form a fleshy common tunic. All individuals work together to ensure the survival of the compound organism.

It is truly remarkable that the simple-looking tunicates are one of the most advanced group of organisms found in the intertidal zone. Animals in the phylum Urochordata have a primitive nerve cord (notochord), and they are distantly related to fish, whales and man.

A unique feature of tunicates is the heart, which reverses its beating every few minutes to change the direction in the flow of blood. Any advantage this system provides is currently unknown.

Purple form with closed siphons.

Orange form with open siphons.

▷ MUSHROOM TUNICATE
Distaplia occidentalis

Other names: Club tunicate; western distaplia.
Description: Extremely variable in color, ranging from white to orange or purple.
Size: Colonies to 5" (12 cm) in diameter. Several colonies may grow together in the same area.
Habitat: Low intertidal zone to subtidal waters 50' (15 m) deep. Often found on floats.
Range: Alaska to San Diego, California.
Notes: The mushroom tunicate is a colonial or social tunicate made up of several individuals. It gets its name from the shape of small colonies when under water. Each member of the colony is called a zooid. Together these zooids produce an oral siphon to admit water into that colony. Smaller, separate siphons pass the water out of the body, once the food has been filtered out. It is believed that this tunicate's high acid content may help protect it from its enemies.

›Brooding Transparent Tunicate

Corella inflata

Other names: Solitary tunicate; transparent tunicate. Early records refer to this species as *Corella willmeriana*, which is now known to be a similar looking, deep-water species.
Description: Clear and colorless, occasionally with small flecks of gold or orange.
Size: To 2" (5 cm) high.
Habitat: On rocks and floats, low intertidal zone to subtidal depths of 65' (20 m).
Range: British Columbia to the San Juan Islands, Washington.
Notes: The internal organs of this solitary tunicate are clearly visible through its outer covering (tunic). This species broods both its eggs and embryos until the larvae have hatched. It is more than 99 percent water, yet it is preyed upon by several animals, including the morning sun star (see p. 131).

›Shiny Red Tunicate

Cnemidocarpa finmarkiensis

Other names: Red sea squirt; broad base tunicate.
Description: Bright red or orange, with 2 equal siphons on top of smooth tunic surface. Broad base attaches to a rock.
Size: To 2" (5 cm) wide, 1" (2.5 cm) high.
Habitat: Attached to rocks in areas with strong currents, low intertidal zone to 165' (50 m) deep.
Range: Alaska to Point Conception, California.
Notes: This solitary sea squirt has been reported to live as deep as 1,782' (540 m) in Japan. It is also found in both the Canadian and European Arctic. It is sometimes seen on rocks covered with many other small organisms. Two crater-like siphons provide the means by which all sea squirts obtain water for both food and respiration. The painted sea star (see p. 134) is a predator.

›STALKED TUNICATE
Styela montereyensis

Other names: Long-stalked sea squirt; Monterey stalked tunicate.

Description: Thick, leathery reddish-orange covering, with several distinctive elongated wrinkles.

Size: To 10" (25 cm) high.

Habitat: On protected and exposed rocky shores, low intertidal zone to water 100' (30 m) deep.

Range: Vancouver Island to Baja California.

Notes: Stalked tunicates found in quiet bays grow to a larger size than those found in exposed locations. One individual has been known to reach 9" (23 cm) in height in 3 years. The top of this tunicate may be pointed straight up or its weight may pull it downward at right angles to the stalk. This species can absorb and store vanadium from its environment (see spiny-headed tunicate, below).

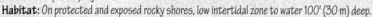

›SPINY-HEADED TUNICATE
Boltenia villosa

Other names: Hairy sea squirt; stalked hairy sea squirt; bristly tunicate.

Description: Red, orange or tan covering with orange to deep red siphons. Spines cover the body, which may or may not be on an elongated stalk.

Size: To 4" (10 cm) high.

Habitat: On hard substances, low intertidal zone to water 330' (101 m) deep.

Range: Prince Rupert, BC to San Diego, California.

Notes: This sea squirt and the stalked tunicate (see above) have been found to separate vanadium (a metal element used in the making of various alloys) from their environment and to concentrate it in their bodies. The leather star (see p. 131) and painted sea star (p. 134) have been known to prey on this tunicate.

›Warty Tunicate
Pyura haustor

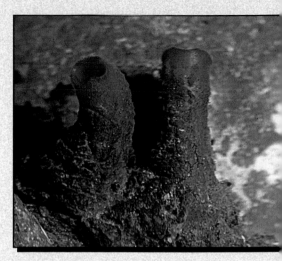

Other names: Solitary sea squirt; wrinkled seapump.
Description: The 2 exposed red siphons are often the only recognizable part of this species. Globular body normally covered with debris and encrusting organisms.
Size: To 3" (7.6 cm) wide.
Habitat: Attached to hard substrates, low intertidal zone to depths of 660' (200 m).
Range: Aleutian Islands, Alaska to San Diego, California.
Notes: The warty tunicate reproduces at all times of the year, when both eggs and sperm are released into the ocean. Like all tunicates, it is a filter-feeder. The striped sun star (see p. 132) is known to prey on this tunicate.

›Compound Tunicates
Various Species

Other names: Compound sea squirt; sea pork.
Description: Color varies from white to yellow, orange or red. A wide variety of fleshy, irregular-shaped colonies can be formed.
Size: To 12" (30 cm) across.
Habitat: On both outer coast and semi-protected rocky shores, low intertidal zone to at least 276' (84 m) deep.
Range: Alaska to Mexico.

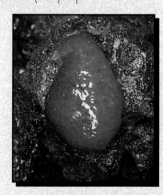

Notes: Compound tunicates are highly organized filter-feeding organisms. Individuals in the colony (zooids) work together to ensure the survival of the entire colony. Both the leather star (see p. 131) and the bat star (p. 130) are known predators of some of these species.

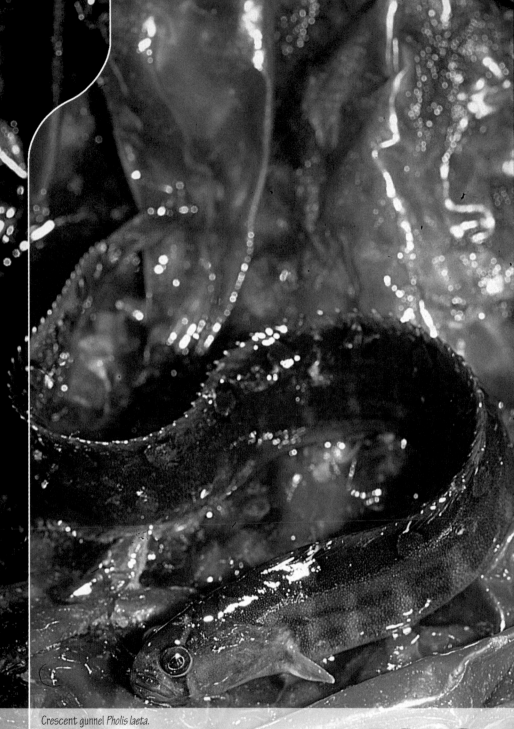

Crescent gunnel *Pholis laeta.*

FISHES
Phylum Chordata

Fishes can be found in all marine habitats from tidepools to deep subtidal waters. Various species have been harvested by man for centuries and are one of our more important foods, but few intertidal species have ever been harvested. A large number of species are found in the intertidal habitat, most of them small and hardy individuals.

▷ SKATE EGG CASES

BIG SKATE *Raja binoculata*

Other names: Pacific great skate; barndoor skate.

STARRY SKATE *Raja stellulata*

Other name: Prickly skate.

Description: Egg case of both species is normally black when found on the beach. Big skate egg case has 2 curved ridges on upper surface and 2 keels on each side with short horns. Starry skate egg case is striated with long horns at each end.

Size: Big skate egg case to 12" (30 cm) long; starry skate egg case to 4" (10 cm) long.

Egg cases of big skate (left) and starry skate.

Habitat: On exposed sandy beaches.

Range: Big skate from Alaska to Mexico; starry skate from Gulf of Alaska to southern California.

Notes: The big skate is our largest skate, growing to a weight of 200 lbs (90 kg). The tidepooler probably won't come across any live skate on the shore; it is much more likely that an empty egg case ("mermaid's purse") will be found there. These light, empty cases are occasionally blown high up on the beach after a storm. Up to 7 eggs are enclosed inside the egg case of the big skate when they are laid, but only 1 egg in the egg case of the starry skate.

▷ NORTHERN CLINGFISH

Gobiesox maeandricus

Other name: Flathead clingfish.

Description: Color varies from light olive to red mottled with darker shades of brown. Distinctive flat head tapers quickly to the tail. **Belly has large circular adhesive disc.**

Size: To 6½" (16 cm) long.

Habitat: Under rocks, often where tidal currents are strong, intertidal to subtidal zones.

Range: Southeastern Alaska to Mexico.

Notes: This fish usually uses its adhesive disc to cling to the underside of a rock, where it waits for food to arrive. Its diet includes the white-lined chiton, lined chiton, shield limpet, plate limpet, ribbed limpet, mask limpet and red rock crab. This fish is also cannibalistic, feeding on sculpins and smaller northern clingfish. If you happen to find this species hiding under a rock, be sure to return the rock to its original position. Many types of invertebrates also make this habitat their home.

▷ TIDEPOOL SNAILFISH

Liparis florae

Other name: Shore liparid.
Description: Color is uniform but varies considerably from brown to green, purple or yellow. This fish is noted for its loose skin. **Small
adhesive disc on belly** acts as a suction
disc to aid the fish in attaching to the underside of rocks.
Size: To 5" (12.7 cm) long.
Habitat: In rocky areas, often among algae or surf-grasses, or attached to the underside of large rocks or
boulders; low intertidal zone to shallow rocky depths.
Range: Bering Sea, Alaska to Point Conception, California.
Notes: The tidepool snailfish can change its color somewhat, turning lighter or darker to match its environment. Its eyes are noticeably small for its size. It feeds primarily on shrimp and similar animals living in its
rocky habitat.

▷ HIGH COCKSCOMB

Anoplarchus purpurescens

Other names: Cockscomb prickleback; crested blenny.
Description: Color varies from brown to olive, purple, orange
or black. **Fleshy crest on top of head.** Light bar normally
present in front of tail fin; no pelvic fins.
Size: To 7³/₄" (20 cm) long.
Habitat: In tidepools and under rocks, intertidal zone.
Range: Aleutian Islands, Alaska to Santa Rosa Island,
California.

Notes: The beachcomber is most likely to find this
fish under an intertidal rock, where several individuals are often grouped together. In the darkness of
night, the high cockscomb comes out from hiding to
feed. Green algae, worms, mollusks and crustaceans
are important foods. Females grow to be larger than
males. They are known to release 2,700 eggs, which
are then guarded and fanned by the female as she
wraps her body around them. The common garter
snake is a predator of this species.

▷ BLACK PRICKLEBACK

Xiphister atropurpureus

Other name: *Epigeichthys atropurpureus*.
Description: Color varies from **reddish brown to black**. Elongated body has 4 lateral lines. Conspicuous **light band is present at base of tail fin**.
Size: To 12" (30 cm) long.
Habitat: Under rocks on exposed shorelines, low intertidal zone.
Range: Kodiak Island, Alaska to northern Baja California.
Notes: The black prickleback feeds on an assortment of algae in addition to a few species of small invertebrates. This species breeds in late winter and spring. The egg mass is typically laid under a rock or similar object, then guarded by the male for about 3 weeks before the eggs hatch. This fish is most often found beneath a rock in little if any water. These damp conditions help keep the fish and other organisms from drying out, so if you turn over any rocks, please replace them carefully.

• •

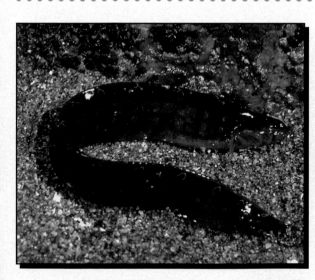

▷ CRESCENT GUNNEL

Pholis laeta

Other name: Bracketed blenny.
Description: Lime-colored on top, lighter below. **Series of crescent-shaped markings along the back**, just below long dorsal fin.
Size: To 10" (25 cm) long.
Habitat: Under seaweed or rocks and in tidepools, mid-intertidal zone to water 240' (73 m) deep.
Range: Bering Sea to northern California.
Notes: This wriggling fish feeds on a variety of small bivalves and nips off the cirri or feeding appendages of barnacles. It wraps its body around its eggs to provide protection from predators until the eggs hatch. It is a common species, which has been known to live as long as 6 years. Mergansers are likely important predators.

• •

▷ SADDLEBACK GUNNEL
Pholis ornata

Other name: Saddled blenny.
Description: Green to brown with elongated body and elongated dorsal and anal fins. **Repeated U-shaped arch pattern along upper body**.
Size: To 12" (30 cm) long.
Habitat: Under rocks or with eel-grass, intertidal zone to subtidal waters 120' (37 m) deep.
Range: Bering Sea to central California.
Notes: The gunnels are a group of fish also frequently referred to as blennies. "Blenny" is a European term for several families of fish which include gunnels, pricklebacks and others. The eggs of the saddleback gunnel are laid in late winter to the first hint of spring and guarded by both parents. The crescent gunnel (above) is similar looking, with crescent-shaped marks along its upper body.

▷ TIDEPOOL SCULPIN
Oligocottus maculosus

Description: Color varies brown to green or reddish on dorsal side, fading to lighter hues on underside.
Size: To 3½" (8.9 cm) long.
Habitat: In tidepools, in nearly any intertidal zone.
Range: Bering Sea to southern California.
Notes: The tidepool sculpin has been well studied by biologists. They have found this species very tolerant of extreme changes in temperature, from the heat of tiny tidepools in direct sun to the cool waters of high tide. This sculpin is able to use its sense of smell to "home" back to its original tidepool if displaced. Scientists have also found this species is capable of changing its color to match its environment.

Plants

Sea hair Enteromorpha *sp.*

SEAWEEDS
Phyla Chlorophyta, Phaeophyta,
Rhodophyta

Seaweeds or marine algae use pigments, such as chlorophyll, to trap energy from the sun and store it as chemical energy in the bonds of a simple sugar (glucose). These plants are an important part of both the intertidal and subtidal ecosystems. Their presence provides food and shelter, as well as oxygen, to the wide variety of invertebrates and vertebrates found here. They are the base to many food webs linked to all species. Seaweeds are classified into three separate groups (phyla), according to the types of pigments present: green algae (phylum Chlorophyta), brown algae (phylum Phaeophyta) and red algae (phylum Rhodophyta).

People all over the world have gathered and eaten seaweeds, probably for hundreds of years. At least 70 species have been harvested from the Pacific Ocean.

GREEN ALGAE
Phylum Chlorophyta
Green algae contain chlorophylls a (a primary photosynthetic pigment in plants that release oxygen) and b (an accessory pigment also found in vascular plants). In this way they are very similar to green land plants. The green algae are found in shallow waters where chlorphyll is most efficient. Green algae store their sugars as starch.

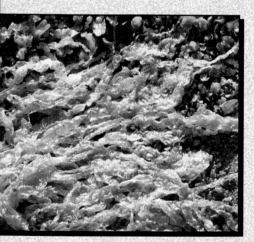

› SEA HAIR
Enteromorpha sp.

Other names: Tube weed; link confetti; formerly *Ulva sp.*
Description: Bright yellowish-green with elongated, unbranched hollow blades.
Size: Normally to 8" (20 cm) long, occasionally to 3.3' (1 m).
Habitat: In rocky areas, upper to mid-intertidal zones and at freshwater seeps. Also an epiphyte on other species of algae (attached to an organism with no harm to that organism), often in tidepools.
Range: Aleutian Islands, Alaska to Mexico.
Notes: Sea hair is often bleached white by the sun. Upon close inspection, its fine tubes appear "hair-like." This seaweed has been used in stews: a small amount flavors a very large volume of stew. Sea hair looks similar to some species of sea lettuce (see below).

>Sea Lettuce
Ulva fenestrata

Other name: Window seaweed.
Description: Light green or darker oblong blade. Smooth surface, often split into broad lobes, with ruffled edge. Several small holes may be present on blades.
Size: To 7" (18 cm) long.
Habitat: Attached to rocks or other species of algae, all intertidal zones. Also found floating on mud flats, lower intertidal zone.
Range: Bering Sea to Chile.
Notes: This alga is very tolerant of a great range of temperatures. It is often found out of water, somewhat dried out, when the tide is low. Under fertile conditions, this species will cover large areas. Similar species of sea lettuce have traditionally been eaten by Hawaiians in a variety of ways, including being mixed with other seaweeds and served with sushi, and being made into a light soup and then mixed into stews. Another species, corkscrew sea lettuce *Ulva taeniata*, has narrow blades in a corkscrew pattern.

>Sea Moss
Cladophora sp.

Description: Bright green with a filamentous shape, growing in low mats.
Size: To 2" (5 cm) high.
Habitat: In rocky areas, mid- to low intertidal zones.
Range: Alaska to Baja California.
Notes: The structure of sea moss enables it to hold large volumes of water, preventing it from drying out when the tide recedes. There are a few different species of sea moss, all growing low to the ground and forming moss-like mats or tufts.

>TANGLE WEED
Acrosiphonia coalita

Other names: Gametophyte stage: green rope;
formerly *Spongomorpha coalita*; **Sporophyte stage:**
formerly *Chlorochytrium inclusum*.
Description: Occurs in 2 separate stages.
Gametophyte stage: bright green with many filaments which become entangled to resemble rope.
Sporophyte stage: tiny greenish spots on red algae.
Size: To 12" (30 cm) tall.
Habitat: On exposed rocky areas, mid- to low intertidal zones.
Range: Alaska to California.
Notes: The rope-like strands of tangle weed occur in
only the gametophyte (sexual) stage of its life cycle. A
spore (saprophyte) produced at this stage lives in the
crustose stage of a few species of red algae, including
papillate seaweed (see p. 173). Tangle weed is some-
times found as an epiphyte, living on another species of algae without harming it. The sporophyte (asexual)
stage is very difficult to find as it is both unicellular and only found within the tissue of various red algae
species.

Sea pearls growing on encrusting coralline algae.

>SEA PEARLS
Derbesia marina

Other name: Globose stage: Formerly *Halicystis ovalis*.
Description: Light to dark green. Occurs in 2 separate
stages. **Globose stage:** greenish to black spherical globules,
especially on encrusting coralline algae (see p. 170).
Filamentous stage: irregularly branched elongated
filaments.
Size: Globose stage: to 3/8" (1 cm) in diameter.
Filamentous stage: to 1 1/2" (4 cm) long.
Habitat: On encrusting coralline algae, sponges and rocks,
in exposed and sheltered situations, low intertidal zone to
water 33' (10 m) deep.
Range: Alaska to Mexico.
Notes: Only after careful laboratory study were the 2 distinct stages of this species determined to belong to the
same marine algae. The globose stage, often referred to as the "Halicystis" stage, is the sexual stage which
produces gametes, while the filamentous stage reproduces by cell division.

>SEA STAGHORN
Codium fragile

Other names: Dead man's fingers; sponge seaweed; felty fingers; green sea velvet.
Description: Dark green to blackish green with many thin, spongy cylindrical branches rising from a basal disc.
Size: To 16" (40 cm) high.
Habitat: Attached to rocks, mid-intertidal to upper subtidal zones. Also often found in large tidepools.
Range: Alaska to Mexico.
Notes: This spongy seaweed resembles a sponge, but there are no green sponges found on the Pacific coast. The sea staghorn is very rich in vitamins and minerals, so it is often used in soups although it is hard to clean. This alga has invaded the New England coast, where it has caused some problems with the shellfish industry: the young plants often start growing on oysters, mussels and scallops, increasing the drag and causing the mollusks to be taken out to sea during storms. A small red algae, staghorn fringe *Ceramium codicola*, lives on sea staghorn and is not found anywhere else.

>SPONGY CUSHION
Codium setchellii

Description: Dark green to black, forming smooth, flat, irregular cushions. Texture varies from firm to spongy as it ages.
Size: To 5/8" (1.5 cm) thick, 10" (25 cm) across; smaller sizes are normally found.
Habitat: In very exposed, rocky areas, often attached to rocks in sandy areas, low intertidal zone.
Range: Sitka, Alaska to Baja California.
Notes: This common, distinctive-looking seaweed is sometimes covered by sand for extended periods.

BROWN ALGAE
Phylum Phaeophyta

Brown algae contain chlorophyll, but the green color is hidden by gold and brown pigments, which look light green to dark black because of the proportions of pigments. Several large brown algae are often referred to as kelp.

› SEA CAULIFLOWER
Leathesia difformis

Other names: Sea potato; *Tremulla difformis*.
Description: Yellow, roughly spherical, convoluted. Hollow and spongy.
Size: To 5" (12 cm) in diameter.
Habitat: In exposed and protected rocky areas, all intertidal zones. Also epiphytic, growing on other species of algae with no harm to the other algae.
Range: Bering Sea to Mexico.
Notes: When this species was first described by the famous botanist Carolus Linnaeus, it was thought to be a jelly fungus because of its unusual shape. The sea cauliflower is solid when young but becomes hollow as it matures. It is found in many parts of the world including Europe, Chile and Sweden.

› FLAT ACID KELP
Desmarestia ligulata

Other names: Acid seaweed; wide desmarestia; flattened acid kelp; formerly *Fucus ligatulus*.
Description: Yellowish brown to dark brown with numerous branches covered in fine hairs. Flat blades attached to a central stalk (stipe).
Size: Normally to 31" (80 cm) long, but has been known to reach 26' (8 m).
Habitat: In rocky areas, low intertidal to upper subtidal zones.
Range: Alaska to South America.
Notes: This species secretes sulphuric acid, which can damage its own tissue as well as other seaweeds. This causes wide-ranging color changes to occur. Stringy acid kelp *Desmarestia viridis*, a closely related acidic species, has fine narrow blades and changes color in similar ways.

› THREE-RIBBED KELP
Cymathere triplicata

Other name: Triple rib kelp.
Description: Color varies from yellow-brown to red-brown. 3 distinct ribs down center of blades.
Size: Blades to 13' (4 m) long, 7" (18 cm) wide.
Habitat: In rocky areas, low intertidal to upper subtidal zones.
Range: Bering Sea to Washington.
Notes: This seaweed smells very much like fresh cucumber, especially when a blade is broken. The author has observed Sitka black-tailed deer (*Odocoileus hemionus sitkensis*) feeding on three-ribbed kelp at low tide (see photo). This deer is also reported to feed on the winged kelp *Alaria marginata* under adverse conditions.

Sitka black-tailed deer feeding on three-ribbed kelp.

› SUGAR KELP
Laminaria saccharina

Other names: Sugar wrack; kombu; oarweed; sea belt.
Description: Long, rich-brown blade with small, stem-like stalk (stipe). Somewhat wrinkled area in mid-blade.
Size: Blades to 11½' (3.5 m) long, 7" (18 cm) wide.
Habitat: In rocky areas, low intertidal to upper subtidal zones.

Range: Alaska to California.
Notes: This common kelp gets its name from the presence of mannite, a sugar alcohol, which gives it a sweet taste. Sea urchins feed on this seaweed. They are believed to find it by detecting a chemical released by the sugar kelp.

❯ SPLIT KELP
Laminaria setchellii

Description: Rich brown to black with prominent stalk (stipe). Blades are split deeply, almost to the ends.
Size: Blades to 32" (80 cm) long, 10" (25 cm) wide.
Habitat: In exposed rocky areas, low intertidal to upper subtidal zones.
Range: Alaska to California.
Notes: The stipe is stiff and stands erect in exposed, surf-swept stretches of the coast. Often this species is found in high enough concentrations to be called an "underwater forest." It is held in place with a very compact holdfast.

Smooth form.

❯ SEA CABBAGE
Hedophyllum sessile

Other name: Formerly *Laminaria sessilis.*
Description: Brown and leather-like with wrinkled blades attached to rock with a sturdy holdfast. Blades become smooth and deeply split in surf-swept areas.
Size: Normally to 20" (50 cm) long; occasionally to 5' (150 cm) long, 32" (80 cm) wide.
Habitat: On rock, mid-intertidal to upper subtidal zones.
Range: Alaska to California.
Notes: This variable species looks completely different in different habitats. Rough waters give it a smooth form while corrugated blades are found in quiet bays and similar habitats.

The black Katy chiton (see p. 61) feeds on the sea cabbage. Sea urchins do not feed on it, so it can become very abundant in areas where urchins are present.

Wrinkled form.

>SEERSUCKER
Costaria costata

Other names: Five-ribbed kelp; ribbed kelp.
Description: Single brown to chocolate-brown blade with 5–7 prominent parallel ribs attached to large stipe.
Size: Blade 20–100" (50–250 cm) long, 4–12" (10–30 cm) wide.
Habitat: In rocky areas and occasionally on wood, low intertidal to upper subtidal zones.
Range: Alaska to California.
Notes: Seersucker is found in sheltered locations and also on the open coast, where it grows somewhat narrower. Tattered and sometimes discolored blades are commonly seen in summer. Sea urchins feed readily on this kelp.

>OLD GROWTH KELP
Pterygophora californica

Description: Dark brown with long, woody stalk (stipe), series of elongated blades originate near the tip.
Size: Stipe to 6.6' (2 m) long, blades to 3' (.9 m) long.
Habitat: In rocky areas, low intertidal zone to water 30' (9 m) deep.
Range: BC to Mexico.
Notes: Old growth kelp has been known to live to 20 years, with new blades growing each year. Its age can be calculated by counting the growth rings of its woody stipe.

> WINGED KELP
Alaria marginata

Other names: Alaria; ribbon kelp.
Description: Olive-brown to rich brown
with prominent linear blade on stipe.
Smaller, wing-like blades (sporophylls) are
attached to the base of the midrib or stipe,
forming a cluster. These produce spores.
Size: Blade 8–10' (2.5–3 m) long, 6–8"
(15–20 cm) wide.
Habitat: In rocky areas, often in areas
exposed to high surf; low intertidal to upper
subtidal zones.
Range: Kodiak Island, Alaska to California.
Notes: Winged kelp has been dried and
used in cooking soups and stews, as a substitute for
kombu (the Oriental species *Laminaria japonica*). It has also
been deep fried and eaten like potato chips, and the midrib
can be eaten fresh in salads, or added to spaghetti sauce.
This is truly a versatile seaweed!

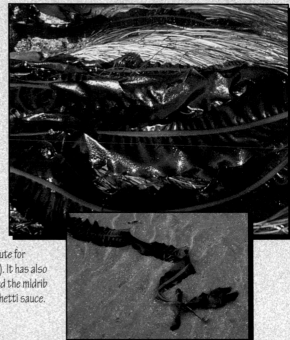

> FEATHER BOA KELP
Egregia menziesii

Description: Color varies from olive green to
brown. Irregular branches along entire stalk (stipe),
and spherical floats often located sparsely along
entire branch. Plant is held securely to rock by a
holdfast.
Size: Branches to 33' (10 m) long, 14" (35 cm)
wide.
Habitat: In rocky exposed areas, low intertidal to
upper subtidal zones.
Range: BC to California.
Notes: This species has been used for many years
as a fertilizer by coastal farmers. The very special-
ized seaweed limpet *Discurria incessa* can sometimes be found feeding on the blades of this seaweed. A close
look is sometimes required to find this limpet.

>Sea Palm
Postelsia palmaeformis

Description: Olive brown, resembles a miniature palm tree. Main stalk (stipe) supports as many as 100 flattened, deeply grooved blades at the tip.
Size: To 24" (60 cm) high, blades to 9" (24 cm) long.
Habitat: In areas exposed to heavy surf, mid- to lower inter-tidal zones.
Range: BC to California.
Notes: This very robust species takes the daily pounding of heavy surf, bouncing back like an elastic band with every wave. The sea palm is an annual, producing spores that germinate close to the parent plant. The shield limpet (see p. 64) can often be found living on the stipe.

>Bull Kelp
Nereocystis luetkeana

Other names: Bullwhip kelp; ribbon kelp.
Description: Up to 20 brown blades attached to a single float which keeps the long stalk (stipe) afloat. Stipe is attached to rock by a sturdy holdfast.
Size: Stipe to 82' (25 m) long, occasionally to 118' (36 m) long; float to $6^{3/4}$" (17 cm) in diameter; blades to 15' (4.5 m) long, to 6" (15 cm) wide.
Habitat: On rocks, upper subtidal zone and lower; also commonly found washed up along beaches after storms.
Range: Alaska to California.
Notes: Bull kelp is one of the largest kelps in the world. Studies in Washington have shown that this species grows $5^{1/2}$" (14 cm) per day. This is truly remarkable—bull kelp is an annual plant and would have grown 82' (25 m) in only one season! Historically, this kelp has been utilized by various peoples, including the Tlingits of Alaska, to make fishing line. The stipe is often used to make pickles. Bull kelp has also been used to make dolls and ornamental musical instruments!

>SMALL PERENNIAL KELP

Macrocystis integrifolia

Other name: Giant kelp.
Description: Well branched. Numerous narrow leaf-like blades, each with a small air bladder or float along the entire length. Holdfast is flattened, closely molded to rock surface.,
Size: To 98' (30 m) long.
Habitat: In rocky areas, very low intertidal zone to water 33' (10 m) deep.
Range: Alaska to California.
Notes: Herring lay their eggs on this kelp, producing a specialty food that is harvested for export to Japan. The air bladders are pickled and used in soups and pizzas, but only occasionally, as this species is found only at the lowest of low tides on exposed coasts. The giant perennial kelp *Macrocystis pyrifera*, a similar species, is larger with a pyramid-shaped holdfast.

>ROCKWEED

Fucus gardneri

Other names: Bladder wrack; popping wrack.
Description: Color varies from olive green to yellowish-green. **Conspicuous midrib**. Flat blades branch regularly and dichotomously along plant.
Size: To 20" (50 cm) high; blades to 5/8" (1.5 cm) wide.
Habitat: Attached to rocks, mid- to low intertidal zones.
Range: Alaska to California.
Notes: Rockweed can withstand both the freezing of winter and the desiccation of summer. The swollen yellow tips or receptacles of this common species contain the gametes for reproduction. When the tide goes out, the receptacles shrink, squeezing out the gametes. When the tide returns, sperm cells are able to find and fertilize the eggs. In protected areas, this seaweed can live for 5 years. Little rockweed (see below) is a closely related species which has no midrib.

>LITTLE ROCKWEED
Pelvetiopsis limitata

Other name: Rockweed.
Description: Generally light green. Flattened blades divide evenly, similar to rockweed (see above), but there is **no midrib**.
Size: 3–7" (8–18 cm) high.
Habitat: On exposed rocky areas, upper intertidal zone.
Range: Vancouver Island to California.
Notes: This kelp is found at such a high intertidal level that it is out of the water more than in water. In fact, it is under water only at the highest of tides.

>NORTHERN BLADDER CHAIN
Cystoseira geminata

Other name: Chain bladder.
Description: Yellowish-brown to dark brown, with long branches and many narrow branchlets which are flattened and fern-like near the base. **"Chains" of air-filled floats** on many of the branchlets which appear to be thickenings on branchlets; last float is pointed.
Size: To 16' (5 m) long.
Habitat: In rocky areas, low intertidal zone to shallow subtidal water.
Range: Bering Sea, Alaska to Oregon.
Notes: The new growth of spring brings the return of the distinctive, bead-like spherical floats. Over the winter months, only the lower portions of this plant remain, making it more difficult to identify. Sargassum (see below) is a similar-looking species with single, round floats.

›SARGASSUM

Sargassum muticum

Other names: Japweed, wireweed.
Description: Yellowish-brown stipe with many branches, small elongated blades and **single, round floats attached individually to stipe.**
Size: To 6½' (2 m) long.

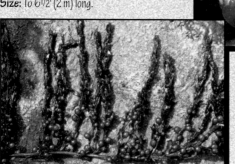

Habitat: In protected rocky areas, low intertidal zone to subtidal water 16' (5 m) deep.
Range: Entire coast.
Notes: Sargassum was accidentally introduced from Japan along with oysters in the 1930s. Since then it has spread along the Pacific coastline. This seaweed is often found washed up on the beach after drifting to shore.

RED ALGAE
Phylum Rhodophyta

Red algae contain chlorophyll, but red and blue pigments are also present, giving these algae a reddish tinge. The life cycle of red algae usually involves three stages, rather than two as in other algae.

›RED FRINGE

Smithora naiadum

Description: Purplish-red to deep purple paper-thin blades.
Size: ¾–4" (2–10 cm) wide.
Habitat: On leaves of surf-grasses (see p. 183) and eel-grasses (p. 183), in intertidal zone.
Range: Alaska to Mexico.
Notes: Red fringe is a distinctive seaweed which is only one cell thick. It is attached to eel-grass or surf-grass by a short, narrow portion of the blade. This delicate seaweed is found most often in late summer and fall, when it is often abundant in tidepools.

>Laver
Porphyra sp.

Other names: Purple laver; red laver; dulse; nori; wild nori.

Description: Color varies from purple to green. Single broad blade, often irregular in shape, has ruffled margins. Often found in dense clusters.

Size: 8–60" (20–150 cm) long.

Habitat: In rocky areas, intertidal to upper subtidal zones. Can be epiphytic (attached to an organism with no harm to that organism) within these zones.

Range: Alaska to Mexico.

Notes: Laver is rubbery and gelatinous in texture, once out of the water. It is edible, and most species are considered to be very tasty as well as having large amounts of vitamins A and C. In Japan, this seaweed is called nori and has been collected and used as food for 1,000 years. Today laver is big business in Japan; its production totals $1 billion annually.

›HAIRY SEAWEED
Cumagloia andersonii

Other name: Formerly *Nemalion andersonii*.
Description: Color varies from brown to purple. Tough, elongated cords, with numerous fibers along the length, hang from rock substrate at low tide.
Size: To 3' (90 cm) tall.
Habitat: On rocks, high intertidal zone.
Range: BC to Baja California.
Notes: This annual species grows back on the same rocks year after year. It reaches its maximum size in August.

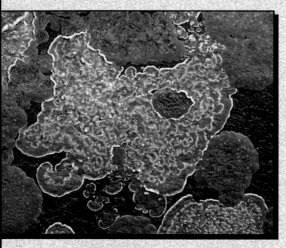

›ENCRUSTING CORALLINE ALGAE
Lithothamnion sp.

Other names: Encrusting coral; rock crust.
Description: Light rose in color. Thin, crust-like shapes resemble lichens.
Size: To 1/16" (2 mm) thick, and can cover large areas.
Habitat: In rocky areas, low intertidal zone to subtidal waters.
Range: Alaska to California.
Notes: Rocks in tidepools and the shells of various gastropods are often covered with this algae. Several invertebrates feed on this species, including northern abalone (see p. 62), whitecap limpet (p. 63) and lined chiton (p. 54).

>BRANCHING CORALLINE ALGAE
Calliarthron sp., Corallina sp., Bossiella sp.

Other name: Coral seaweed.
Description: Color ranges from pink to deep purple. All species have jointed segments which may or may not be noticeably calcified and may be branched in a feather-like fashion.
Size: To 5½" (14 cm) long.
Habitat: In rocky areas, low intertidal to upper subtidal zones, and in tidepools.
Range: Alaska to Mexico.
Notes: The several related species in this group are very similar in appearance. Discovering this unique and beautiful group of seaweeds is an adventure in itself. A 10X hand lens is a valuable tool for examining them in detail.

>NAIL BRUSH SEAWEED
Endocladia muricata

Other name: Sea moss.
Description: Color ranges from dark red to black or greenish-brown. Long filaments, covered with tiny spines, grow in tufts.
Size: To 1½–3" (4–8 cm) tall.
Habitat: On rocks, high intertidal zone.
Range: Alaska to Mexico.
Notes: The name of this alga describes it very well. It is often locally common on the tops and sides of larger rocks. It is a hardy species, able to withstand long periods out of water.

› BROAD IODINE SEAWEED

Prionitis lyallii

Other names: Iodine seaweed; Lyall's iodine seaweed.
Description: Color ranges from dull brown to reddish-purple. Small root-like holdfast holds the flattened blade and bladelets attached along the margin.
Size: To 14" (35 cm) long.
Habitat: On rocks in tidepools, mid-intertidal zone and deeper into upper subtidal zone. Coarse sand often covers the rock this species attaches to.
Range: Alaska to Mexico.
Notes: This seaweed smells like bleach. It is often found in sandy areas.

› SUCCULENT SEAWEED

Sarcodiotheca gaudichaudii

Other names: Formerly *Agardhiella tenera*; *Neoagardhiella baileyi*; *Neoagardhiella gaudichaudii*.
Description: Color varies from pink to red. **Slender, somewhat fleshy branches** and many branchlets tapering to sharp points.
Size: To 16" (40 cm) long.
Habitat: In rocky areas, low intertidal zone to subtidal waters 60' (18 m) deep, and sometimes in tidepools.
Range: Alaska to Chile.
Notes: This common species often grows in clumps.

>TURKISH TOWEL
Chondracanthus corymbiferus

Other names: Formerly *Gigartina corymbifera*; *Mastocarpus corymbiferus*.
Description: Brick red to purplish-red blades, often iridescent when under-water. Blade surface is covered with tiny rasp-like projections.
Size: To 20" (50 cm) long, 8" (20 cm) wide.
Habitat: Lower intertidal zone to water 65' (20 m) deep.
Range: BC to California.
Notes: This species is a source of carrageenan, a stabilizer for a wide range of products including cottage cheese and printer's ink, and has been experimentally farmed to produce this substance.

>PAPILLATE SEAWEED/SEA TAR
Mastocarpus papillatus

Other names: Crust stage: Sea tar; tar spot; sea film; formerly *Petrocelis franciscana*; *Petrocelis middendorffii*. **Blade stage:** Crisp leather; Turkish washcloth; formerly *Gigartina papillata*, *Gigartina cristata*.
Description: Crust stage: Dark, red-brown to black smooth crust grows on rock. **Blade stage:** Upright, smooth blade ranging in color from yellow-brown to dark purple or even black. Blades are palm-like in shape, normally with several branches. Flat, irregularly branched blades later develop small growths or projections.
Size: Crust stage: to 3.3' (1 m) in diameter. **Blade stage:** to 6" (15 cm) tall.
Habitat: In rocky areas, high intertidal (near rockweed) to low intertidal zones.
Range: Alaska to Mexico.
Notes: This highly variable species had scientists mystified for years. It was originally thought that the 2 distinct stages were separate species. Only in the last few years was it discovered both stages were part of the same life cycle. The crust stage reproduces asexually to produce spores, which develop into the blade stage. Blades are either male or female and reproduce sexually. Studies have shown that the crustose stage of this alga grows at an extremely slow rate, about 1/2" (1.3 cm) per year, and that larger specimens could be the incredible age of 90 years old.

Crust stage.

❯ IRIDESCENT SEAWEED
Mazzaella splendens

Other names: Rainbow seaweed; formerly *Iridophycus splendens, Iridaea cordata.*

Description: Blades vary in color from green to bluish-purple. Blades often have a split or lobbed shape, and appear iridescent in sunlight.

Size: Blades to 12" (30 cm) long, occasionally to 3' (1 m).

Habitat: In rocky, exposed areas, low intertidal zone to water 23' (7 m) deep.

Range: Alaska to California.

Notes: This striking species is often remembered thanks to its dazzling iridescence, which is especially vivid when touched with sunlight underwater. Various snails feed on it, which is why several holes are sometimes found on the blades of this unmistakable algae.

❯ SEA SACS
Halosaccion glandiforme

Other names: Dead man's fingers; sea sacks; salt sacs; sea nipples.

Description: Color varies considerably from yellowish-brown to olive brown and reddish-purple. Long, hollow sacs are attached in clusters.

Size: To 12" (30 cm) long, sacs to 1½" (4 cm) in diameter.

Habitat: On both exposed and protected rocky areas, mid-intertidal zone.

Range: Aleutian Islands, Alaska to Point Conception, California.

Notes: Young sea sacs are normally purple, and slowly change to light yellow as they grow older. Sea water normally fills or nearly fills each sac when they are submerged. A portion of this water is released through tiny pores when the tide recedes.

> RED FAN
Neoptilota asplenioides

Other names: Sea fern; formerly *Ptilota asplenioides*.

Description: Red in color with fern-like or fan-like shape, with many branches.

Size: To 12" (30 cm) tall.

Habitat: Low intertidal to upper subtidal zones.

Range: Alaska to northern Washington.

Notes: This beautiful species is sometimes collected and dried for decoration, but it is not abundant so this practice is not encouraged. This species, like several other seaweeds, requires additional study to learn more about its natural history.

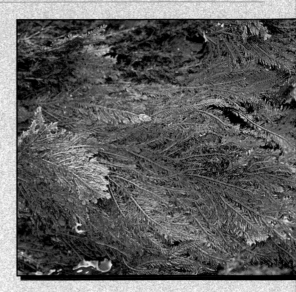

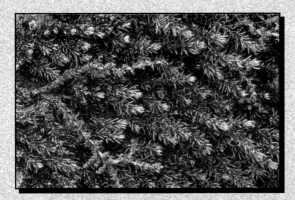

> BLACK PINE
Neorhodomela larix

Other name: Formerly *Rhodomela larix*.

Description: Distinctive brownish-black color. Round branches and branchlets in a uniform cylindrical shape. Clusters often grow from the same attachment point.

Size: To 12" (30 cm) long.

Habitat: In rocky areas, low intertidal zone.

Range: Bering Sea to California.

Notes: This species thrives on rock in sandy, exposed situations such as the outer coast and in exposed rocky tidepools. Here it can grow into mats of many individuals. It is also more tolerant of sediment than other seaweeds.

Golddust lichen
Chrysothrix chlorina.

SEASHORE LICHENS
Phylum Ascomycotina

The phylum Ascomycotina (sac fungi) includes both lichens and cup fungi (but not true fungi). Lichens are a unique working partnership between two organisms: an algae component that photosynthesizes, much as higher plants do, and a fungus, which provides protection. Lichens reproduce both asexually and sexually. There are two common fruiting bodies (sexual reproduction) in maritime lichens: apotheca (disk-like structures) and perithecia (tiny sacs embedded in the thallus, or body).

⟩WAXY FIREDOT
Caloplaca l. luteominia

Other name: *Caloplaca laeta.*
Description: Orange plant body (thallus), abundant orange disc-like fruiting bodies (apothecia).
Size: Patches to 3/4" (2 cm) in diameter, often merging with others to cover larger areas.
Habitat: On rocks, above salt spray zone.
Range: Vancouver Island to California.
Notes: This species is crust-like, lacking any leaf-like structures. It has 2 color phases, the common one (as pictured) with orange apothecia, and a less common phase with crimson apothecia. The waxy firedot prefers exposed sites without bird droppings. It also occurs in the Coast Mountains to at least 2,640' (800 m) elevation.

⟩SMOOTH SEASIDE FIREDOT
Caloplaca rosei

Other name: Rose's orange lichen.
Description: Yellow to orange-yellow upper body (thallus) portion, orange lower portion. Thallus is distinctly cracked and disc-like structures (apothecia) are sparse.
Size: Patches to 1 1/2" (4 cm) in diameter, often merging with others to cover larger areas.
Habitat: On seashore rocks, above salt spray zone, just above black seaside lichen (see p. 181). Exposed sites are generally avoided.
Range: Queen Charlotte Islands, BC to Baja California.
Notes: The smooth seaside firedot can be found on a wide range of rock including volcanic, slate, sandstone and granite. Those lichens found growing on rock with bird droppings are very well developed.

▷ GOLDDUST LICHEN

Chrysothrix chlorina

Other name: Formerly *Lepraria chlorina*.
Description: Yellow to yellow-green, composed almost entirely of small granules (soredia).
Size: Covering rock in areas several square yards in size.
Habitat: On acid rocks, above salt spray zone, in shaded locations. It favours overhangs which are sheltered from the rain.
Range: BC to California.
Notes: The golddust lichen does not produce fruiting bodies (apothecia). Instead it reproduces entirely by spreading powdery granules. This lichen is not restricted to the seashore: it can be found in boreal situations (including locations in Europe) and, more rarely, on the bark of conifers.

▷ MEALY SUNBURST LICHEN

Xanthoria candelaria

Other names: Flame lichen; shrubby orange lichen; shining orange lichen; formerly *Teloschistes lychneus*; *Xanthoria lychnea*.
Description: Bright yellow body (thallus), varying to orange, covered with short leaf-like growths. Disc-like structures (apothecia) are rare.
Size: Patches to 1¹/₄" (3 cm) in diameter, often merging with others to cover larger areas.
Habitat: On rocks, in salt spray zone.
Range: BC to California.
Notes: The mealy sunburst lichen is not restricted to seaside sites. It is found at elevations to 6,000' (1,800 m), on various trees and occasionally on mosses. This lichen is often found on rocks with bird droppings, as it benefits from the nutrients in the droppings.

WHITE-AND-BLACK BUTTON LICHEN

Diplotomma alboatrum

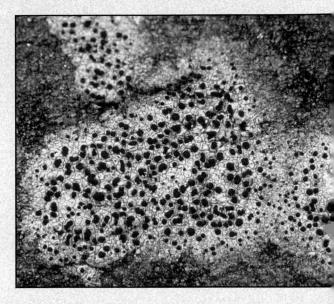

Other names: Tree toad lichen; *Buellia alboatra*; *Rhizocarpon alboatrum*.
Description: White to grayish-white crust-like body (thallus) with black discs (apothecia). Species often has a powdery appearance.
Size: Circular patches to 2" (5 cm) in diameter.
Habitat: On rocks, in salt spray zone.
Range: BC to California.
Notes: The habitat of this lichen is not restricted to the seashore. It is also found on the trunks of a variety of trees. On rocks, it commonly displays a blackish border on the outer edge.

SHORE SHINGLE LICHEN

Fuscopannaria maritima

Other names: Matted lichen; seaside mouse; formerly *Pannaria maritima*.
Description: Brown, somewhat shiny upper body (thallus), white or tan lower body. Bluish-white lobe tips are felt-like. Lacks ball-like structures (soredia).
Size: Covers extended areas of rock surface.
Habitat: On seashore rocks.
Range: Alaska to Oregon.
Notes: This crustose lichen often goes unnoticed because it prefers shaded sites and lacks the bright colors of other species. Its name comes from the tiny scales which make up the thallus.

▷ HOODED ROSETTE LICHEN
Physcia adscendens

Description: Gray and foliose (leafy), tending to lie flat against the substrate. Hood-shaped swellings at tips bear very small, powdery ball-like structures (soredia). (A hand lens will aid greatly in seeing these.)
Size: Rosettes to 2" (5 cm) in diameter.
Habitat: On granite or limestone rocks, in salt spray zone.
Range: Pacific Northwest.
Notes: The distinctive shape of this hooded lichen has been compared to a miniature snake with its head poised and its tongue flicking out. It is a common species, found in agricultural and urban areas, and on the bark and twigs of a wide variety of trees at low elevations.

▷ BLUE ROSETTE LICHEN
Physcia caesia

Other names: Blue-gray rosette lichen; gray rock lace; blue-gray blister lichen.
Description: Color varies blue-gray to grayish-white, often with brown or black discs. Foliose (leafy) bodies often found in patches with distinct lobes.
Size: Rosettes to 3" (8 cm) in diameter.
Habitat: On granite or calcareous rocks in beach areas, above salt spray zone.
Range: Circumpolar in the northern hemisphere.
Notes: This lichen is found in a number of habitats besides the beach. It is so adaptable it is even found in alpine regions.

>SEASIDE TARSPOT LICHEN

Verrucaria epimaura

Description: Dark black when wet, yellowish-brown to black when dry. Body (thallus) is thick and lobed, often circular.
Size: Patches to 1" (2.5 cm) or more in diameter.
Habitat: On rocks, in salt spray zone.
Range: Alaska to Vancouver Island.
Notes: The seaside tarspot lichen was described as a new species of lichen in 1997. This species is found only along the coastline of the Pacific Northwest. Unlike some lichen species, which simply tolerate the salt spray, this species requires it. The seaside tarspot lichen is sometimes found growing over the black seaside lichen (see below).

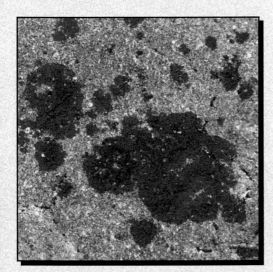

>BLACK SEASIDE LICHEN

Verrucaria maura

Other names: Black lichen; blackish blind lichen; "sea tar."
Description: Black when in the sun, various shades of gray when out of the sun, gelatinous when wet. Thin, smooth surface changes to cracked patches around the fruiting bodies (perithecia). Fruiting bodies are often not visible, or form slight pimple-like elevations on the body.
Size: Patches to 4" (10 cm) in diameter, more commonly in near-continuous strips to 39" (1 m) wide, along shoreline.

Habitat: On rocks, high intertidal to lower salt spray zones.
Range: Bering Sea to California.
Notes: The black seaside lichen clings tightly to its rock. It is often easier to see from a distance than close up. This is a very common lichen, also found on the Atlantic coast in Maine, Massachusetts and Rhode Island. The Sitka periwinkle (see p. 69) and checkered periwinkle (p. 70) are believed to feed on this **tar-like** lichen.

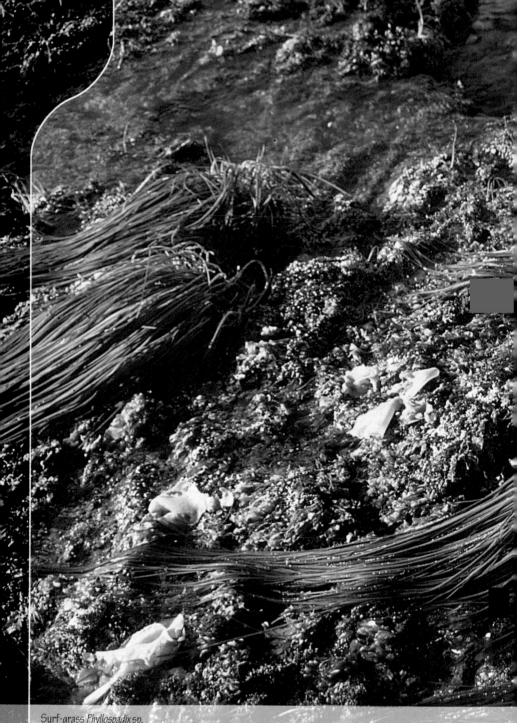

Surf-grass *Phyllospadix* sp.

FLOWERING PLANTS
Phylum Anthophyta

The flowering plants found in the intertidal zone lack the bright colors of flowering plants elsewhere, but they provide an important habitat for a wide array of both invertebrates and vertebrates (fish).

> SURF-GRASS
Phyllospadix sp.

Other name: Surfgrass.
Description: Long, wiry blades with oval or round cross-section.
Size: Leaves normally to 60" (150 cm) long, blade to 1/8" (4 mm) wide.
Habitat: On rock in exposed areas, low intertidal to upper subtidal zones.
Range: Alaska to Mexico.
Notes: This common plant is found in just about all open coast sites. It provides food and shelter to many other plant and animal species. The sweet rhizomes of both surf-grass and eel-grass (see below) were traditionally eaten fresh or dried for the winter by both the Salish and Haida.

> EEL-GRASS
Zostera sp.

Other name: Eelgrass.
Description: Long, flat blades. Roots grow in mud.
Size: Leaves normally to 8' (2.5 m) long, 1/2" (1.2 cm) wide.
Habitat: In quiet bays with mud bottom, low intertidal zone to water 100' (30 m) deep.
Range: Alaska to Mexico.
Notes: Like surf-grass, this is a species on which many other plants and animals depend for food and shelter. People have harvested the seeds of this species as they harvest wheat.

Best Beachcombing Sites in the Pacific Northwest

There are hundreds of public sites in the Pacific Northwest that are rich in intertidal life, as well as being beautiful and enjoyable places to explore. A few favorite sites with easy access have been included here. Wherever you go to observe our many fascinating marine animals and plants, please remember that these sites are wild yet fragile natural areas. Look out for your own safety, and for the safety of the living things of the seashore.

Key to Site Descriptions

 **Exposed** Subjected to the direct action of waves

 Semi-exposed Somewhat sheltered from large waves

 Protected Not subjected to the full force of wave action

 Sand Mostly sand deposited on a beach

 Mud Primarily a mud base, in sheltered areas, with a low volume of sand

 Sand/Mud Mixture of sand and mud

 Gravel Accumulation of small rocks or pebbles

 Rock Predominantly bedrock, rocky outcrops, boulders and/or rocks

 Tidepools Having one or more pools of salt water, varying in size, once the tide goes out

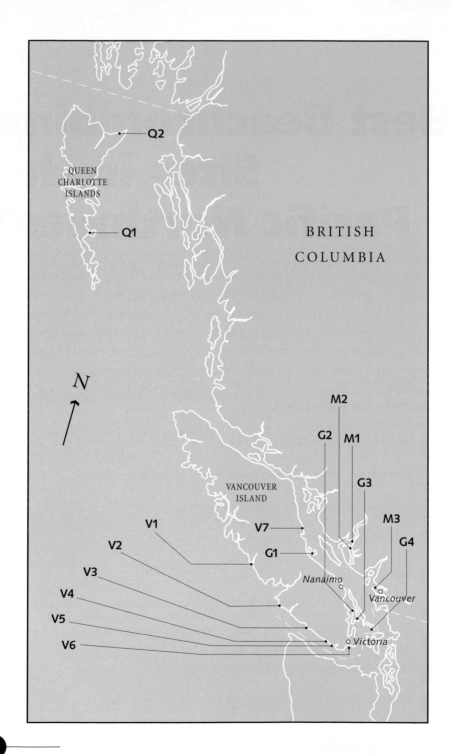

Intertidal Sites in British Columbia

Queen Charlotte Islands (Haida Gwaii)

Q1 . . . . Burnaby Narrows
Q2 . . . . Yakan Point

Vancouver Island

V1 . . . . Pacific Rim National Park
V2 . . . . Bamfield
V3 . . . . Botanical Beach Provincial Park
V4 . . . . French Beach Provincial Park
V5 . . . . Whiffen Spit Regional Park
V6 . . . . East Sooke Regional Park
V7 . . . . Miracle Beach Provincial Park

Gulf Islands

G1 . . . . Tribune Bay Provincial Park, Hornby Island
G2 . . . . Montague Harbour Provincial Marine Park, Galiano Island
G3 . . . . Winter Cove Provincial Marine Park, Saturna Island
G4 . . . . Beaver Point, Ruckle Provincial Park, Salt Spring Island

Mainland

M1 . . . . Saltery Bay Provincial Park
M2 . . . . Skookumchuck Narrows Provincial Park
M3 . . . . Stanley Park, Vancouver

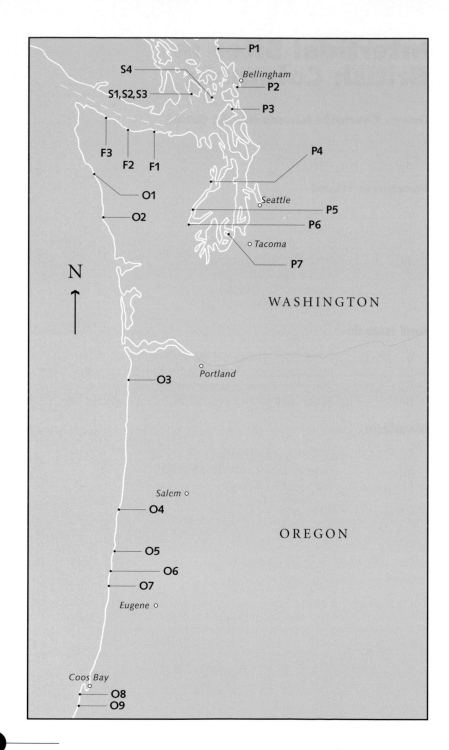

Best Beachcombing Sites in the Pacific Northwest

P1

S4

Bellingham

P2

S1, S2, S3

P3

F3

F2 F1

P4

O1

Seattle

P5

O2

P6

Tacoma

P7

N

WASHINGTON

O3

Portland

Salem

O4

OREGON

O5

O6

O7

Eugene

Coos Bay

O8

O9

Intertidal Sites in Washington & Oregon

Puget Sound Area

P1. . . . . Birch Bay State Park
P2 . . . . Larrabee State Park
P3 . . . . Deception Pass State Park, Rosario Bay
P4 . . . . Dosewallips State Park, Hood Canal
P5 . . . . Tacoma Public Utilities Salt Water Park, Hood Canal
P6 . . . . Potlatch State Park, Hood Canal
P7 . . . . Penrose Point State Park, Carr Inlet

San Juan Islands

S1 . . . . False Bay, San Juan Island
S2 . . . . Cattle Point, San Juan Island
S3 . . . . Lime Kiln Point State Park, San Juan Island
S4 . . . . Spencer Spit State Park, Lopez Island

Strait of Juan de Fuca

F1. . . . . Tongue Point (Salt Creek Recreation Area)
F2 . . . . Pillar Point County Park
F3 . . . . Slip Point

Outer Coast, Washington

O1. . . . . Hole-In-The-Wall, Olympic National Park
O2 . . . . Beach 4, Olympic National Park

Outer Coast, Oregon

O3 . . . . Ecola State Park
O4 . . . . Devil's Punch Bowl State Natural Area
O5 . . . . Seal Rock State Wayside
O6 . . . . Cape Perpetua Scenic Area
O7 . . . . Neptune State Park
O8 . . . . Sunset Bay State Park
O9 . . . . Cape Arago State Park

BRITISH COLUMBIA

British Columbia is fortunate to have a wonderful mixture of exposed and sheltered intertidal sites within its boundaries. The long, intricate coastline and the many islands of all sizes provide a rich mix of habitats in which the beachcomber can observe a spectacular variety of flora and fauna, at almost any time of the year.

Queen Charlotte Islands (Haida Gwaii)

   ## BURNABY NARROWS (DOLOMITE NARROWS)

Site description: Protected, sand/mud, rock.
Nearest town: Sandspit, Queen Charlotte Islands.
Access: This remote site, located in Gwaii Haanas National Park Reserve, is accessible only by boat or organized tour (kayak or sailboat), and the number of visitors to this site is limited. To make reservations or to contact one of the several tour operators, write to the address below.
Notes: A visit to Burnaby Narrows is truly a memorable experience. This is a rich intertidal area—indeed, it is often difficult to walk without stepping on some living thing—but it is also a fragile ecosystem. As its name indicates, the area is a shallow, narrow channel of water located between Burnaby Island and Moresby Island. **Bat stars** (see p. 130) are very common and can be seen in every imaginable color. Other local inhabitants include the **giant plumose anemone** (p. 41), **red turban** (p. 67), **Lewis's moonsnail** (p. 72) and **red rock crab** (p. 120). Many intertidal species can be found beneath the abundant **seaweeds** produced at this site.
For more information: Write to Superintendent, Gwaii Haanas National Park Reserve, P.O. Box 37, Queen Charlotte City, BC V0T 1S0 Canada. Tel: (604) 559-8818. Web site: http://parkscanada.pch.gc.ca

    ## YAKAN POINT, GRAHAM ISLAND

Site description: Exposed, sand, rock, tidepools.
Nearest town: Masset, Queen Charlotte Islands.
Access: From Queen Charlotte City, drive north on Highway 16 to Masset, then east along the highway toward Tow Hill. Park at the Agate Beach campground of Naikoon Provincial Park. Yakan Point lies just west of this campground, on the north shore of Graham Island.

Notes: Great variety awaits those who visit this diverse site. **Painted anemones** (see p. 39) are often seen hanging from their rock substrate in a most obscene manner here, and rocky outcrops can also harbor the **red turban** (p. 67), **Pacific blood star** (p. 132) and **sunflower star** (p. 135). The **California sea cucumber** (p. 140) and **Dungeness crabs** (p. 121) can often be found on the sand or in tidepools. Great numbers of **fat gaper** (see p. 91) shells accumulate with the wave action here, indicating the prolific nature of this area.

This intertidal site lies on First Nations lands. Please be courteous while visiting.

For more information: Write to Queen Charlotte Island Information Centre, 3220 Wharf Street, P.O. Box 819, Queen Charlotte City, BC V0T 1S0 Canada. Tel: (250) 559-8316.

Vancouver Island

  PACIFIC RIM NATIONAL PARK RESERVE

Site description: Exposed, sand, rock.
Nearest town: Tofino, Vancouver Island.
Access: From Port Alberni, drive east on Highway 4 about 65 miles (115 km).
Notes: This national park reserve is a wonderful place to explore intertidal life on the exposed coast of

Vancouver Island. Situated in the northwest portion, **LONG BEACH** is a magnificent stretch of sandy beach facing the open ocean. The fine sand here is home to **Pacific razor-clams** (see p. 93) and **Pacific lugworms** (p. 49), while the **purple olive** (p. 77) is often seen plowing just under the surface of the sand at low tide. A host of other creatures live in the area around **BOX ISLAND** and **WICKANINNISH**, two rocky intertidal sites at either end of Long Beach. The presence of the **sea palm** (p. 165) and **goose barnacle** (p. 107) indicate the exposed nature of Box Island.

For more information: Write to Superintendent, Pacific Rim National Park Reserve, Box 280, Ucluelet, BC V0R 3A0 Canada. Tel: (250) 726-7721. Web site: http://parkscanada.pch.gc.ca. Visit: Wickaninnish Visitor Centre (in the park).

BAMFIELD

Site description: Exposed, sand, rock.
Nearest town: Port Alberni, Vancouver Island.
Access: Follow the signs and take the gravel road south from Port Alberni, about 50 miles (84 km). To make sure you find your way, stay on the road with power lines.
Notes: There are several sites to visit in the Bamfield area. **PACHENA BAY** is an easy-to-reach spot featuring a fabulous sandy beach. Here you may find both the **purple olive** (see p. 77) and the shells of **expanded macoma** (see p. 94).
BRADY'S BEACH is a rocky intertidal site on Mills Peninsula, a separate section of Bamfield. **Bat stars** (p. 130), **flattop crabs** (p. 114), **morning sun stars** (p. 131), **leather stars** (p. 131) and many other intertidal species can be found here. A vehicle is not necessary to reach Mills Peninsula, and seeing it on foot is best anyway. Just follow the signs. **Services are limited in Bamfield. Please take supplies with you.**
For more information: Write to Bamfield Chamber of Commerce, P.O. Box 5, Bamfield, BC V0R 1B0 Canada. Tel: (250) 728-3006.

   BOTANICAL BEACH PROVINCIAL PARK

Site description: Exposed, rock, tide-pools.
Nearest town: Port Renfrew, Vancouver Island.
Access: From Victoria, take Highway 14 , a winding road on the west coast of Vancouver Island, to Port Renfrew. From Port Renfrew, follow the signs along the gravel road, about 2 miles (3 km) to the Botanical Beach parking area. From there, a 30-minute hike will take you to the intertidal site. Just follow the signs.
Notes: Botanical Beach features sandstone outcrops which have been shaped and molded over the years by the power of the ocean. Impressive surge channels and many tidepools of varying sizes have also formed, providing habitats for a list of species so extensive that the area has been an academic study area for many years. Species found here include the **rough keyhole limpet** (see p. 62), **hooked slipper-snail** (p. 71), **red nudibranch** (p. 81), **goose barnacle** (p. 107), and **sea palm** (p. 165).
For more information: Write to BC Parks, South Vancouver Island District, 2930 Trans-Canada Highway, Victoria, BC V9E 1K3 Canada. Tel: (250) 391-2300.

French Beach Provincial Park

Site description: Exposed, rock, tidepools.
Nearest town: Sooke, Vancouver Island.
Access: From Sooke, drive west on Highway 14 about 12 miles (21 km).
Notes: From the shore of this beautiful park, you can look out to the Strait of Juan de Fuca. The molded sandstone tidepools harbor several species, including the **plate limpet** (see p. 64) and **hairy chiton** (p. 55). The rocky areas are rich with marine life such as the **red nudibranch** (p. 81) and **Monterey dorid** (p. 81). Be sure to check beneath the wealth of seaweeds attached to the many and varied rocks. A campground is located in this park.
For more information: Write to BC Parks, South Vancouver Island District, 2930 Trans-Canada Highway, Victoria, BC V9E 1K3 Canada. Tel: (250) 391-2300.

   # East Sooke Regional Park

Site description: Exposed, sand, rock.
Nearest town: Sooke, Vancouver Island.
Access: From Sooke, drive east on Highway 14 for about 5 miles (8 km). Turn south on Gillespie Road and follow the road until you reach a T-intersection at East Sooke Road. Turn either way to find a parking

lot. The east parking area can be reached by taking Betcher Bay Road, while the west is located near the end of East Sooke Road. Both parking areas have site maps showing hiking trails.
Notes: This popular park protects a large area of shoreline rich with seaweeds and intertidal species, including the **plumose anemone** (see p. 40), **Olympia oyster** (p. 87), **channelled dogwinkle** (p. 74) and **graceful decorator crab** (p. 118). Several miles of trails have been developed along the water and through the forest areas. These trails provide a sure and easy way to reach the shoreline with its several small beaches. The forest is mainly Douglas-fir, with many arbutus along the shore.
For more information: Write to Sooke Region Museum & Travel InfoCentre, Box 774, Sooke, BC V0S 1N0 Canada. Tel: (250) 642-6351.

WHIFFEN SPIT REGIONAL PARK

Site description: Semi-exposed, sand/mud, rock.
Nearest town: Sooke, Vancouver Island.
Access: From Sooke, drive west on Highway 14, turn south on Whiffen Spit Road and drive about 1 mile (1.5 km) to the parking lot.

Notes: This semi-exposed site experiences a good deal of wave action, and invertebrates and marine algae thrive on the exposed side of the spit. A wide variety of crabs are often found here, including the **helmet crab** (see p. 120) and **red rock crab** (p. 120). You may also see the **proliferating anemone** (p. 37), **red-beaded anemone** (p. 38) and **mushroom tunicate** (p. 144), as well as **river otters** and **harbor seals**. A trail running along the spit takes you back to the parking area.
For more information: Write to Sooke Region Museum & Travel InfoCentre, Box 774, Sooke, BC V0S 1N0 Canada. Tel: (250) 642-6351.

  ## MIRACLE BEACH PROVINCIAL PARK

Site description: Protected, sand.
Nearest town: Courtenay, Vancouver Island.
Access: From Courtenay, drive north on Highway 19 about 11 miles (18 km).
Notes: This park offers a large, pleasant sandy beach for bathers, beachcombers and sand-castle builders of all ages. This is a good spot to see **moonglow anemones** (see p. 34) and **Pacific gapers** (p. 92), which often squirt jets of water into the air unexpectedly and with uncanny accuracy! **Great blue herons** are often seen here as well, waiting quietly for their next meal. A campground and nature house are open during the summer months.
For more information: Write to BC Parks, Strathcona District, P.O. Box 1479, Parksville, BC V9P 2H4 Canada. Tel: (604) 954-4600.

Gulf Islands

 BEAVER POINT, RUCKLE PROVINCIAL PARK,
SALTSPRING ISLAND

Site description: Protected, rock.
Nearest town: Fulford, Saltspring Island.
Access: From the Fulford Harbour ferry terminal, drive west along Beaver Point Road about 6 miles (10 km).
Notes: Beaver Point is an easily accessible site with a mixture of intertidal species, including the **painted anemone** (see p. 39), **yellow-edged nudibranch** (p. 80), **flattop crab** (p. 114), **Pacific blood star** (p. 132) and **six-rayed star** (p. 133). A great variety of seaweeds can also be seen. This is a sheltered site but care should be taken here, as boat traffic can create unexpected waves.
For more information: Write to BC Parks, South Vancouver Island District, 2930 Trans-Canada Highway, Victoria, BC V9E 1K3 Canada. Tel: (250) 391-2300.

  MONTAGUE HARBOUR PROVINCIAL
MARINE PARK, GALIANO ISLAND

Site description: Protected, sand, rock.
Nearest town: Sturdies Bay, Galiano Island.
Access: Drive along Montague Road about 5 miles (8 km) from the ferry terminal at Sturdies Bay. The route is well signed and easy to follow, and the park is just off the road.
Notes: Montague Harbour, one of the few marine parks that can be reached by vehicle, is a pleasant mixture of forest and seashore. Limited camping is permitted here, in a forest campground situated amidst Douglas-fir, arbutus and bigleaf maple. This is a rich and varied intertidal site with many species found on, between and under the rocks. Look for the **moonglow anemone** (see p. 34), **plumose anemone** (p. 40), **fat gaper** (p. 91), **red rock crab** (p. 120) and **mottled star** (p. 133). There is also an impressive **shell beach**, indicating which clams are buried here. Large shell middens left generations ago by Salish people have also been found here. If you plan to harvest shellfish, be aware of closures, limits and license requirements.
For more information: Write to BC Parks, South Vancouver Island District, 2930 Trans-Canada Highway, Victoria, BC V9E 1K3 Canada. Tel: (250) 391-2300.

WINTER COVE PROVINCIAL MARINE PARK, SATURNA ISLAND

Site description: Protected, sand/mud, rock, tidepools.
Nearest town: Lyall Harbour, Saturna Island.
Access: From the ferry terminal at Lyall Harbour, drive along East Point Road for about 2¹/₂ miles (4.5 km) (keep to the left), turn left at Winter Cove Road and drive about ¹/₃ mile (.5 km) to reach the parking area.

Notes: The shoreline of Winter Cove park produces **Pacific oysters** and a variety of **clams**, and the rocky areas are the habitat of several other species. At least 5 species of sea stars can be found here, including the **giant pink star** (see p. 134) and **sunflower star** (p. 135). The **striped anemone** (p. 41) can also be found in the tidepools. If you take a short walk northwest along the trail, an extended bedrock area awaits you with a series of tidepools. This rocky area, at the edge of the Strait of Georgia, is a great spot to explore, but the point is too steep and slippery to visit.

Early risers may catch a glimpse of a **river otter** at the water's edge. In the spring, **Steller's sea lions** and **California sea lions** may also be heard from a small island nearby. **No public camping is allowed on Saturna Island**. Book other accommodations well in advance.

For more information: Write to BC Parks, South Vancouver Island District, 2930 Trans-Canada Highway, Victoria, BC V9E 1K3 Canada. Tel: (250) 391-2300; or SuperNatural BC Information and Reservations, tel: (800) 663-6000.

TRIBUNE BAY PROVINCIAL PARK, HORNBY ISLAND

Site description: Protected, sand.
Nearest town: Denman Village, Denman Island.
Access: From Buckley Bay south of Courtenay on Vancouver Island, take the ferry to Denman Island, then another ferry to Hornby Island. A short drive along the main road takes you to Tribune Bay.
Notes: Hornby Island, quiet and peaceful by nature, is one of the northern Gulf Islands. The beautiful white sandy beach at Tribune Bay is especially popular with sunbathers during the summer months, and

there is a campground in the park. In this idyllic setting, **eccentric sand dollars** can be seen by the hundreds in these sheltered waters. Look for several seaside **lichens** on the water-sculpted sandstone rocks on either side of the beach.

For more information: Write to BC Parks, Strathcona District, P.O. Box 1479, Parksville, BC V9P 2H4 Canada. Tel: (604) 954-4600.

Mainland of British Columbia

   SALTERY BAY PROVINCIAL PARK

Site description: Protected, sand, mud, rock.

Nearest town: Powell River.

Access: From the Saltery Bay ferry terminal, drive northwest along Highway 101 for .6 mile (1 km).

Notes: This park boasts 2 intertidal sites. **MERMAID COVE** is a well-known dive site adjacent to the campground with a paved walkway/ramp down to the water's edge. The area has a great mud beach with large boulders to explore. The clam digger will delight in the various **clams**. (Be sure to check limits and closures first.) The **fat gaper** (see p. 91) and the distinctive egg cases of the **Lewis's moonsnail** (p. 72) can often be found here. A short drive farther along Highway 101 is a **PICNIC AREA**, where a fabulous sandy beach awaits those who visit at low tides. Here the **leather star** (p. 131), **mottled star** (p. 133) and **eccentric sand dollar** can often be seen.

For more information: Write to BC Parks, Garibaldi/Sunshine Coast District, P.O. Box 220, Brackendale, BC V0N 1H0 Canada. Tel: (604) 898-3678.

Skookumchuck Narrows Provincial Park

Site description: Semi-exposed, rock.
Nearest town: Egmont, Sunshine Coast.

Access: From Sechelt, drive north on Highway 101 toward Egmont and follow the signs to the parking lot. A pleasant 1-hour walk along a beautiful, well-marked wooded trail takes you to the intertidal sites, the best of which are located on the way to and including Rowland (North) Point.

Notes: This area is a sheltered one but is famous for the turbulent waters that funnel through Skookumchuck Narrows as the tide comes and goes into Sechelt Inlet. Tides occur approximately 100 minutes later than shown on the tide table for Point Atkinson (check local newspapers for local tide times). Noteworthy species to be found on and under the rocks here are the **Northern horse mussel** (see p. 86), **hairy crab** (p. 113) and **green sea urchin** (p. 138), as well as the **red sea urchin** (p. 139), often in both the red and purple color phases. Several chitons, including **Merten's chiton** (p. 58), **white-lined chiton** (p. 55), **woody chiton** (p. 56), **Swan's mopalia** (p. 57), **black Katy chiton** (p. 61), and **giant Pacific chiton** (p. 61) also inhabit this area.

For more information: Write to BC Parks, Garibaldi/Sunshine Coast District, P.O. Box 220, Brackendale, BC VON 1H0 Canada. Tel: (604) 898-3678.

   # Stanley Park

Site description: Protected, sand/mud, rock.
Nearest town: Vancouver.
Access: This park is situated at the end of the downtown peninsula in Vancouver, just off Highway 1 south of the Lions Gate bridge. Well-placed signs in Vancouver allow easy access. Various roads and parking areas in the park provide access to several intertidal areas and to several public beaches.
Notes: Stanley Park is a large urban park with a magnificent mixture of mature forest, cultivated gardens, lakes and seashore where a multitude of recreational pursuits are enjoyed. Douglas-fir, bigleaf maple and western redcedar flourish in the mature forest, and the seawall promenade circling the park

provides 5.5 miles (8.8 km) of shoreline along which to observe a wide variety of marine life. Several intertidal sites are located along the seawall, including **THIRD BEACH** and **BROCKTON POINT**. The many creatures waiting to be discovered here include the **mask limpet** (p. 66), **Nuttall's cockle** (see p. 91), **dark mahogany-clam** (p. 95), **acorn barnacle** (p. 105) and **yellow shore crab** (p. 123).

For more information: Write to Stanley Park, Board of Parks & Recreation, 2099 Beach Avenue, Vancouver, BC V6G 1Z4 Canada. Tel: (604) 257-8400.

WASHINGTON

The coastline of Washington is rich with intertidal sites. Rugged exposed shores are the home of organisms that thrive on the constant movement of water, while the many sheltered areas provide habitats for the flora and fauna that require protected enironments. Some sites in Puget Sound are subjected to a total tidal amplitude (the difference between very low and high tides) of some 15 feet (4.5 m), compared to 9 feet (2.7 m) in other coastal areas.

Puget Sound Area

   BIRCH BAY STATE PARK

Site description: Protected, gravel, rock.
Nearest town: Blaine.
Access: From Blaine, drive south on Highway 548 about 7 miles (11 km) and follow the signs. Or take exit 266 or 270 from Interstate 5 and follow the signs for 8 miles (13 km).
Notes: This park has an extended gravel beach where **Nuttall's cockle** (see p. 91), **Japanese littleneck** (p. 97) and other hardshell clams can be found. Interpretive signs assist those who are unfamiliar with local species. **Dungeness crab** (p. 121) and **red rock crab** (p. 120) can also be seen here. If you are lucky enough to visit in the springtime, you may observe **brant** feeding on eel-grass along the shoreline. These geese merely stop here to feed and rest during their spring migration.

For more information: Write to Washington State Parks and Recreation Commission, 7150 Cleanwater Lane, P.O. Box 42650, Olympia, WA 98504-2650 USA. Tel: (800) 233-0321.

LARRABEE STATE PARK

Site description:
Protected, rock.
Nearest town:
Bellingham.
Access: Take Interstate 5 to exit 250 and follow the signs on Highway 11 for approximately 8 miles (13 km).
Notes: This state park offers a wonderful blend of ocean, freshwater lakes, a coastal forest of Douglas-fir and western redcedar and a total of 8,100 feet (2,430 m) of shoreline. Here you can observe a wide variety of sea creatures, including the **plumose anemone** (see p. 40) and **six-rayed star** (p. 133). Look carefully under the rocks and in the few small tidepools to discover many other creatures. Be sure to return all rocks to their original positions.
For more information: Write to Washington State Parks and Recreation Commission, 7150 Cleanwater Lane, P.O. Box 42650, Olympia, WA 98504-2650 USA. Tel: (800) 233-0321.

   ## DECEPTION PASS STATE PARK

Site description: Protected, rock, sand.
Nearest town: Oak Harbor.
Access: From Oak Harbor, drive north on Highway 20, about 9 miles (14 km).
Notes: Deception Pass State Park is an excellent mix of temperate rain forest, freshwater lakes and seashore. Recreationists enjoy camping, hiking, boating, swimming, fishing and diving. In fact, this impressive park is one of the busiest in the state. Deception Pass divides this park into two halves. In the north portion lies **ROSARIO BEACH**, an easy-to-reach intertidal site. This is a seemingly sheltered site, but many of the species found here show some evidence of exposure to rough water. Look for the **painted anemone** (see p. 39), **black Katy chiton** (p. 61) and **orange sea cucumber** (p. 141), among many other species.
For more information: Write to Washington State Parks and Recreation Commission, 7150 Cleanwater Lane, P.O. Box 42650, Olympia, WA 98504-2650 USA. Tel: (800) 233-0321.

DOSEWALLIPS STATE PARK, HOOD CANAL

Site description: Protected, sand/mud.
Nearest town: Brinnon.
Access: From Brinnon, drive south on Highway 101 for 1 mile (1.6 km).
Notes: This park is a haven for oysters and clams, including the **Pacific oyster** (see p. 88), **Nuttall's cockle** (p. 91), **butter clam** (p. 96), **Japanese littleneck** (p. 97) and **softshell-clam** (p. 98). Be sure to check for seasons, closures and bag limits if you plan to harvest shellfish. A viewing tower with interpretive signs relating to the tidal flats is located at the beach.
For more information: Write to Washington State Parks and Recreation Commission, 7150 Cleanwater Lane, P.O. Box 42650, Olympia, WA 98504-2650 USA. Tel: (800) 233-0321.

TACOMA PUBLIC UTILITIES SALT WATER PARK, HOOD CANAL

Site description: Protected, sand/mud.
Nearest town: Potlatch.
Access: From Potlatch, drive south on Highway 101 for 1 mile (1.6 km).
Notes: This is an excellent site for the **Pacific oyster** (see p. 88). Be sure to check for seasons, closures and bag limits, if you plan to harvest shellfish. Other species found here include the **red rock crab** (p. 120) and **mottled star** (p. 133). Intertidal fish such as the **high cockscomb** (p. 150) can also be found, hiding beneath larger rocks. Remember to carefully return all rocks to their original positions.
For more information: Write to Washington State Parks and Recreation Commission, 7150 Cleanwater Lane, P.O. Box 42650, Olympia, WA 98504-2650 USA. Tel: (800) 233-0321.

POTLATCH STATE PARK, HOOD CANAL

Site description: Protected, sand/mud.
Nearest town: Shelton.
Access: From Shelton, drive north on Highway 101, 12 miles (19 km).
Notes: Many beaches along Hood Canal are open to the public and have much to offer beachcombers and shellfish enthusiasts. **Pacific oysters** (see p. 88) abound in most of these sites. Be sure to check for seasons, closures and bag limits. To explore these sites fully, check beneath rocks or gently dig a hole or two in the sand. Especially low tides may yield some unexpected results! Potlatch State Park is a great site for several shellfish, including the **butter clam** (p. 96) and **Japanese littleneck** (p. 97).
For more information: Write to Washington State Parks and Recreation Commission, 7150 Cleanwater Lane, P.O. Box 42650, Olympia, WA 98504-2650 USA. Tel: (800) 233-0321.

   ## PENROSE POINT STATE PARK, CARR INLET

Site description: Protected, sand/mud, rock.
Nearest town: Gig Harbor.

Access: From Tacoma, drive north along Highway 16 for about 2.5 miles (4 km) and exit to Highway 302. Follow the signs to the park (which is 3.5 miles/5.5 km south of the town of Home) on the Key Peninsula Highway.
Notes: This state park is home to a great variety of species. In shallow waters at low tide, you may well see **rough piddock** (see p. 100), with excellent views of their siphons in action. Clam and oyster diggers can harvest the **Pacific oyster** (p. 88), **butter clam** (p. 96) and **Pacific littleneck** (p. 96). The **red rock crab** (p. 120) is common here as well, and the distinctive burrows of **bay ghost shrimp** (p. 112) are plentiful at this site.
For more information: Write to Washington State Parks and Recreation Commission, 7150 Cleanwater Lane, P.O. Box 42650, Olympia, WA 98504-2650 USA. Tel: (800) 233-0321.

San Juan Islands

  ### FALSE BAY, SAN JUAN ISLAND

Site description: Protected, mud.
Nearest town: Friday Harbor, San Juan Island.
Access: Travel west on Spring Street in Friday Harbor, about 1¹/2 miles (2.5 km) to False Bay Road. Turn left and drive 3¹/2 miles (5.6 km) to the parking area.
Notes: This area and its marine life are protected as a University of Washington biological preserve. False Bay is an excellent example of a mud beach scattered with rocks and boulders. To find many of the inhabitants here, carefully turn a few rocks. If you take your time, you will see many more creatures. **Sitka periwinkles** (see p. 69) hide in the shade while **yellow shore crabs** (p. 123) scatter from beneath rocks. The antics of **hairy hermits** (p. 117) can also be watched here. Other local species include **Nuttall's cockle** (p. 91), **bent-nose macoma** (p. 95), **Pacific littleneck** (p. 96) and **soft-shell-clam** (p. 98). If you move any rocks, please return them to their original positions.
For more information: Write to University of Washington Marine Field Laboratories, 620 University Road, San Juan Island, WA 98250 USA. Tel: (360) 378-2165.

    ### CATTLE POINT, SAN JUAN ISLAND

Site description: Semi-exposed, sand, rock, tidepools.
Nearest town: Friday Harbor, San Juan Island.
Access: Travel west on Spring Street in Friday Harbor. Turn south on Mullis Road, which becomes Cattle Point Road and eventually leads you to the site.
Notes: Cattle Point is a combination of stabilized dunes and intertidal area, protected by the Washington Department of Natural Resources. The most interesting intertidal sites will be found by working your way along the shoreline, toward the lighthouse. This is a semi-exposed coastal area, where you can find **goose barnacles** (see p. 107), indicating an area with stronger waves, as well as other species such as the **aggregating anemone** (p. 35) and **yellow shore crab** (p. 123) which normally inhabit more sheltered areas. A variety of seaweeds may also be washed ashore, especially after a storm. They come from lower subtidal waters, having been torn from their holdfasts when these waters are churned up. The light at Cattle Point is a landmark that mariners have used for many years, especially in the fog of Strait of Juan de Fuca.
For more information: Write to the Department of Natural Resources, Aquatic Resources Division, Natural Resources Building, 1111 Washington Street SE, P.O. Box 47027, Olympia, WA 98504-7027 USA. Tel: (800) 527-3305.

LIME KILN POINT STATE PARK, SAN JUAN ISLAND

Site description: Protected, rock.
Nearest town: Friday Harbor, San Juan Island.

Access: In Friday Harbor, travel west on Spring Street to Douglas Road. Turn south and follow Douglas Road to the park. The name of this road changes first to Bailer Hill Road, then to West Side Road. The total distance is about 8 miles (13 km).

Notes: The rocky shores and bluffs of this park are best explored when tides are at their very lowest and the more uncommon species become visible. **Checkered periwinkles** (see p. 70) are particularly noticeable here, with a distinctive checkered pattern on their shells. Look for the **rough keyhole limpet** (p. 62), **whitecap limpet** (p. 63), **blue topsnail** (p. 69) and **wrinkled amphissa** (p. 76). This park is also a favorite dive site, as well as a good viewpoint for observing **Minke and killer whales** and **Dall's and harbor porpoises** from June through September. Interpretive signs aid in identifying these marine mammals.

For more information: Write to Washington State Parks and Recreation Commission, 7150 Cleanwater Lane, P.O. Box 42650, Olympia, WA 98504-2650 USA. Tel: (800) 233-0321.

  # SPENCER SPIT STATE PARK, LOPEZ ISLAND

Site description: Protected, sand.
Nearest town: Lopez Village, Lopez Island.
Access: From the ferry terminal, drive south on Ferry Road to Stanley Road. Turn east and follow Stanley Road, a winding road, for a short distance. Turn east onto Baker View Road, which leads to the park.

Notes: The state park on this friendly, quiet island offers a sand beach attractive to beachcombers and clam diggers alike. Look for the **fat gaper** (see p. 91), **bent-nose macoma** (p. 95), **Pacific littleneck** (p. 96), **Japanese littleneck** (p. 97) and **softshell-clam** (p. 98). A newcomer, the **dark mahogany-**

clam (p. 95), is now found at this park as well, having made its way from the Strait of Georgia in British Columbia, where it was accidentally introduced from Japan. Spencer Spit park also has a saltwater marsh lagoon that attracts a variety of birds, including the **belted kingfisher, great blue heron, Canada goose, northern pintail, bufflehead** and **mallard**.
For more information: Write to Washington State Parks and Recreation Commission, 7150 Cleanwater Lane, P.O. Box 42650, Olympia, WA 98504-2650 USA. Tel: (800) 233-0321.

Strait of Juan de Fuca

  TONGUE POINT

Site description: Exposed, rock.
Nearest town: Port Angeles.

Access: From Port Angeles, drive west on Highway 117 and take Highway 112 west toward Joyce. The Salt Creek Recreation Area is about 8 miles (13 km) along. There are two points of access: one at the campground of Salt Creek Recreation Area, and the other at a wildlife viewing parking area farther along the highway.

Notes: Allow plenty of time while visiting Tongue Point—it is a large area and something new waits for you at every turn. Several nudibranchs, including the **cryptic nudibranch** (see p. 78), **orange-spotted nudibranch** (p. 80), **red nudibranch** (p. 81), **Monterey dorid** (p. 81), **ringed nudibranch** (p. 82), **frosted nudibranch** (p. 83), **opalescent nudibranch** (p. 83) and **shaggy mouse nudibranch** (p. 84) have all been observed here. The presence of **California mussels** (p. 85) and **goose barnacles** (p. 107) indicate that this is an area of strong waves.
For more information: Write to Clallam County Parks & Fair Department, 223 East 4th Street, Port Angeles, WA 98362 USA. Tel: (360) 417-2291.

SLIP POINT

Site description: Exposed, rock, gravel, tidepools.
Nearest town: Port Angeles.
Access: From Port Angeles, drive west on Highway 117, then take Highway 112 west, about 40 miles (64 km) to Clallam Bay. Turn right at Frontier Street and travel for less than 1 mile (1 km) until reaching Salt Air Street. At the time of writing (1998), this site was administered by the Coast Guard, the Slip Point Light Station was in operation, and the authorities were considering turning the site and its historical buildings into a maritime museum. Ask around locally or contact the address below for an update, and for information on access.
Notes: Slip Point is a rocky point with a large variety of intertidal life in many tidepools and rock edges. **Purple sea urchins** (see p. 138) can be found by the hundreds. A close look at rocks may reveal the **painted anemone** (p. 39), **veiled-chiton** (p. 60), **California datemussel** (p. 87) and **flat-tip piddock** (p. 100). The **red ribbon worm** (p. 44) and **red-beaded anemone** (p. 38) can often be observed in tidepools. This site is also locally well known for various marine fossils.
For more information: Write to Clallam County Parks & Fair Department, 223 East 4th Street, Port Angeles, WA 98362 USA. Tel: (360) 417-2291.

    PILLAR POINT COUNTY PARK

Site description: Protected, sand, rock, tidepools.
Nearest town: Clallam Bay.
Access: From Port Angeles, drive west on Highway 112, about 35 miles (56 km).
Notes: Clam diggers and tidepool enthusiasts enjoy this large, protected bay with **eel-grass** beds. Watch carefully and you may spot a **purple star** (see p. 135) feeding on clams, which are abundant. Some of the **Pacific gapers** (p. 92) here reach an immense size. You may also see a **Dungeness crab** (p. 121), or several other species of crabs. Look for the **moonglow anemone** (p. 34), **aggregating**

anemone (p. 35), **frilled dogwinkle** (p. 74) and **thatched barnacle** (p. 104) in the sand or on boulders.
For more information: Write to Clallam County Parks & Fair Department, 223 East 4th Street, Port Angeles, WA 98362 USA. Tel: (360) 417-2291.

Outer Coast

HOLE-IN-THE-WALL, OLYMPIC NATIONAL PARK

Site description: Exposed, sand, rock.
Nearest town: Forks.
Access: From Forks, drive west on Highway 110 to Rialto Beach in Olympic National Park. From this parking area, you can reach Hole-in-the-Wall by walking north along the beach for about an hour. You will come to one small stream along the way, but it is easily crossed.
Notes: A walk on this wonderful beach is well worth the time spent in reaching the area. The site is as easily identified as its name suggests. It is a picturesque site and an excellent location to watch the antics of **grainyhand hermits** (see p. 116) in tidepools. Keep a close watch for nudibranchs, including the **Monterey dorid** (p. 81), **opalescent nudibranch** (p.83) and **shaggy mouse nudibranch** (p. 84), and for the **black turban** (p. 67) and **Pacific blood star** (p. 132). Guided walks are offered daily in the park during the summer months. This is an excellent opportunity to learn more about the intertidal plants and animals in the area.
For more information: Write to Superintendent, Olympic National Park, 600 East Park Avenue, Port Angeles, WA 98362 USA. Tel: (360) 452-4501. Web site: http:www.nps.gov.

   ### BEACH 4, OLYMPIC NATIONAL PARK

Site description: Exposed, rock, tidepools.
Nearest town: Forks.
Access: From Forks, drive south on Highway 101, about 26 miles (42 km).
Notes: Beach 4, once known as Starfish Point, is an excellent location to observe the **purple star** (see p. 135) in high numbers, often with the **giant green anemone** (p. 36). The presence of the **goose barnacle** (p. 107) indicates the rocky, exposed nature of this coast. The power of the water is also evident in

the smooth sandstone shapes, some of which form tidepools at low tide. These landforms have been sculpted over thousands of years. Guided walks are offered daily in the park during the summer months, often at this site.
For more information: Write to Superintendent, Olympic National Park, 600 East Park Avenue, Port Angeles, WA 98362 USA. Tel: (360) 452-4501. Web site: http:www.nps.gov.

OREGON

Oregon is graced with many intertidal sites that are exposed to the rough waters of the Pacific. The Department of Fish and Wildlife has recognized the importance of this resource and has protected many of these sites, designating some intertidal sites as "marine gardens." Many of these sites, and others as well, offer interpretive presentations and guided walks, most during spring and summer, on low tide weekends. This is an excellent way to explore and enjoy intertidal areas. For more information on Oregon's rocky intertidal areas, contact Oregon Department of Fish and Wildlife, Marine Resources Program, 2040 Marine Science Drive, Newport, OR 97365 USA, telephone (503) 867-4741.

   ## ECOLA STATE PARK

Site description: Exposed, sand, rock.
Nearest town: Cannon Beach.

Access: From Cannon Beach, take Highway 101 north. Just follow the signs to the park, a short distance away. The intertidal area is easily reached at **INDIAN BEACH**.
Notes: This popular state park has a rich, varied intertidal area with both fine sandy beaches and impressive boulder areas. **Purple olives** (see p. 77) and **Pacific mole crabs** (p. 118) are easily spotted on sandy beaches. In rocky areas, look for the **Monterey dorid** (p. 81), **giant barnacle** (p. 105) and **goose barnacle** (p. 107). As in all exposed areas, keep a close watch on the water—don't be surprised by an unexpected wave, or log.
For more information: Write to Oregon Parks and Recreation Department, 1115 Commercial Street NE, Salem, OR 97310-10001 USA. Tel: (800) 551-6949.

    ## DEVIL'S PUNCH BOWL STATE NATURAL AREA

Site description: Exposed, sand, rock, tidepools.
Nearest town: Newport.
Access: From Newport, drive north on Highway 101 for 9 miles (14.5 km). Follow the signs to Devil's Punch Bowl and to Otter Rock, the intertidal site.
Notes: This extensive rocky intertidal area includes **OTTER ROCK**, which has been declared a "marine garden" by Oregon's Department of Fish and Wildlife. **Purple sea urchins** (see p. 138) occur here in very

high numbers, each in its own rock depression. Tidepools hold such treasures as **rufus tipped nudibranch** (p. 79) and **mossy chiton** (p. 56). The area is also rich in marine algae. You may also observe **harbor seals** hauled out on the rocks. Please exercise caution to ensure the safety of these and all marine mammals.

For more information: Write to Beverly Beach State Park, 198 NE 123 Street, Newport, OR 97365 USA. Tel: (541) 265-9278.

   ## SEAL ROCK STATE WAYSIDE

Site description: Exposed, rock, tidepools.
Nearest town: Newport.
Access: From Newport, drive south on Highway 101 for 12 miles (19 km). Seal Rock State Wayside is just off the highway.
Notes: Upturned basalt rock forms the base for the offshore islands, making an impressive backdrop for this area. The presence of the **sea palm** (see p. 165) indicates this is an area of high surf, while tidepools and shallow submerged sandstone flats make for great exploring. At least three types of nudibranchs live here: the **Monterey dorid** (p. 81), **ringed nudibranch** (p. 82) and **opalescent nudibranch** (p. 83). The **Arctic hiatella** (p. 99) inhabits the rock cavities made by rock-boring clams in the area.

Watch for **harbor seals** hauled out on the rocks, from which the site gets its name.

For more information: Write to Oregon Parks and Recreation Department, 1115 Commercial Street NE, Salem, OR 97310-10001 USA. Tel: (800) 551-6949.

CAPE PERPETUA SCENIC AREA

Site description: Exposed, rock, tidepools.
Nearest town: Yachats.

Access: From Yachats, drive south on Highway 101 for 2 miles (3 km). Most activities begin at the interpretive center.

Notes: Cape Perpetua has been officially declared one of Oregon's "marine gardens." Here visitors can view surge channels and the **sea palm** (see p. 165), which indicates an area of very high surf. Look for the **black turban** (p. 67), **goose barnacle** (p. 107), **striped shore crab** (p. 122) and **purple sea urchin** (p. 138). Cape Perpetua Interpretive Center offers a range of services, including guided walks—an excellent way to learn about the plants and animals of the area. *Exercise caution* when visiting all intertidal areas, especially those exposed to the coast.

For more information: Write to Cape Perpetua Interpretive Center, Box 274, Yachats, Oregon, 97498 USA. Tel: (514) 547-3289.

   NEPTUNE STATE PARK

Site description: Exposed, sand, rock.
Nearest town: Yachats.

Access: From Yachats, drive south on Highway 101, about 4 miles (6 km).

Notes: At **STRAWBERRY HILL**, a rocky intertidal "marine garden," at least one university is currently conducting intertidal studies. Look for the **giant green anemone** (see p. 36), **rough piddock** (p. 100), **black turban** (p. 67), **goose barnacle** (p. 107) and **sunflower star** (p. 135). You may also see marine mammals, including **harbor seals, California sea lions, Steller's sea lions** and **elephant seals**. Exercise care in viewing these mammals. If approached, they may abandon their haulout.

For more information: Write to Oregon Parks and Recreation Department, 1115 Commercial Street NE, Salem, OR 97310-10001 USA. Tel: (800) 551-6949.

SUNSET BAY STATE PARK

Site description: Protected, sand, rock, tidepools.
Nearest town: Charleston.
Access: From Charleston, drive south along the coast on the Cape Arago Highway, about 1 mile (1.6 km).
Notes: This protected site has a solid rock base, with tidepools in which many marine creatures hide. The **black turban** (see p. 67) and **opalescent nudibranch** (p. 83) are just two of these. The **red-beaded anemone** (p. 38) can be found in the shallows here. **California beach hoppers** (p. 109) can often be observed the first thing in the morning, before the sun comes out and they hide for the day. Check the beach at the high tide mark, among the bits of seaweed left from the last high tide. As the park's name implies, this is a great spot to sit back and watch a fabulous sunset.
For more information: Write to Oregon Parks and Recreation Department, 1115 Commercial Street NE, Salem, OR 97310-10001 USA. Tel: (800) 551-6949.

 ## CAPE ARAGO STATE PARK

Site description: Exposed, sand, rock, tidepools.
Nearest town: Charleston.
Access: From Charleston, drive south along the coast on the Cape Arago Highway, for 2 miles (3 km). The highway ends at Cape Arago State Park.
Notes: Cape Arago State Park features three excellent sites: **NORTH COVE, MIDDLE COVE** and **SOUTH COVE**. Take care in hiking to these sites, as the trails are subject to erosion over time. Seaweed is especially abundant here—so slippery at times that it is a challenge to stay upright, but the algae shelter a wealth of marine creatures. The **purple olive** (see p. 77), **red nudibranch** (p. 81) and **Monterey dorid** (p. 81) inhabit this area, and a close look at local tidepools may reveal the **red ribbon worm** (p. 44), **giant Pacific chiton** (p. 61), **umbrella crab** (p. 112) and **sunflower star** (p. 135). The presence of **goose barnacles** (p. 107) and **purple sea urchins** (p. 138) indicate the exposed nature of these sites. Researchers from the University of Oregon have studied in the Cape Arago area for many years.
For more information: Write to Oregon Parks and Recreation Department, 1115 Commercial Street NE, Salem, OR 97310-10001 USA. Tel: (800) 551-6949.

Further Reading

Behrens, David W. 1991. *Pacific Coast Nudibranchs: A Guide to the Opisthobranchs Alaska to Baja*. Monterey, CA: Sea Challengers.

Harbo, R. M. 1997. *Shells & Shellfish of the Pacific Northwest: A Field Guide*. Madeira Park, BC: Harbour Publishing.

_____ 1999. *Whelks to Whales: Coastal Marine Life of the Pacific Northwest*. Madeira Park, BC: Harbour Publishing.

Gotshall, Daniel W. 1994. *Guide to Marine Invertebrates Alaska to Baja California*. Monterey, CA: Sea Challengers.

Jensen, Gregory C. 1995. *Pacific Coast Crabs & Shrimps*. Monterey, CA: Sea Challengers.

Kozloff, Eugene N. 1996. *Marine Invertebrates of the Pacific Northwest*. Seattle, WA: University of Washington Press.

Lamb, A. and P. Edgell. 1986. *Coastal Fishes of the Pacific Northwest*. Madeira Park, BC: Harbour Publishing.

Lambert, P. 1997. *Sea Cucumbers of British Columbia, Southeast Alaska and Puget Sound*. Royal British Columbia Museum Handbook. Vancouver, BC: UBC Press.

O'Clair, R. M. and C. E. O'Clair. 1998. *Southeast Alaska's Rocky Shores: Animals*. Auke Bay, AK: Plant Press.

O'Clair, R. M., S. C. Lindstrom and I. R. Brodo. 1996. *Southeast Alaska's Rocky Shores: Seaweeds and Lichens*. Auke Bay, AK: Plant Press.

Ricketts, Edward F., and Jack Calvin. 1985. *Between Pacific Tides*. Stanford, CA: Stanford University Press.

Snively, Gloria. 1987. *Exploring the Seashore in British Columbia, Washington and Oregon*. Vancouver, BC: Gordon Soules Book Publishers Ltd.

Acknowledgments

I would like to thank the many people who assisted with this project in so many ways.

First I would like to thank Howard White of Harbour Publishing for taking on this project and directing its production. I would also like to thank Peter Robson for his assistance, Mary Schendlinger for her careful editing and Martin Nichols for his great design.

Andy Lamb (Vancouver Public Aquarium, Vancouver, BC) graciously undertook scientific editing, as well as many slide identifications and confirmations. Sandra Millen (University of British Columbia, Vancouver, BC) generously gave of her time and expertise to edit the text on nudibranchs, confirm accompanying slide identifications and assist me in photographing mollusks at the UBC invertebrate museum.

I would also like to thank the following specialists who aided in identifying or confirming identifications, and in many instances added additional information: Roland C. Anderson (Seattle Aquarium, Seattle, WA), Bill Austin (Marine Ecology Station, Cowichan Bay, BC), Irwin M. Brodo (Canadian Museum of Nature, Ottawa, ON), Roger N. Clark (Klamath Falls, OR), Matthew Dick (Middlebury College, Middlebury, VT), Doug Eernisse (California State University, Fullerton, CA), Trevor Goward (Clearwater, BC), Rick Harbo (Fisheries & Oceans, Nanaimo, BC), Mike Hawkes (University of British Columbia, Vancouver, BC), Gregory C. Jensen (University of Washington, Seattle, WA), Gretchen Lambert (Seattle, WA), Philip Lambert (Royal British Columbia Museum, Victoria, BC), Val Macdonald (Victoria), Pamela Roe (California State University, Stanislaus, Turlock, CA) and Ron Shimek (Montana).

In addition, I would like to thank the following institutions for their help with site information and planning: Bamfield Marine Station; British Columbia Parks; Oregon Parks & Recreation Department; Olympic National Park, Washington; Seattle Aquarium; and Washington State Parks and Recreation Commission.

Jeff Goddard (Oregon Institute of Marine Biology, Charleston, OR), Catherine Po (Vancouver Public Aquarium, Vancouver, BC) and Jim Salt (Victoria, BC) kindly gave me site suggestions and other useful information.

Fuji Photo Film Canada provided this project with a generous film sponsorship.

I would especially like to thank my son Dusty Sept for accompanying me on many of my field trips to the seashore. His keen interest, enthusiasm and sharp eyes are a welcome addition to each and every trip.

Index

white sea jelly (moon jelly *Aurelia labiata*), 32
white-and-black button lichen (*Diplotomma alboatrum*), 179
whitecap limpet (*Acmaea mitra*), 63
white-lined chiton (*Tonicella insignis*), 55
white-lined dirona (frosted nudibranch *Dirona albolineata*), 83
white-plumed anemone (giant plumose anemone *Metridium giganteum*), 41
white-plumed anemone (plumose anemone *Metridium senile*), 40
white-spotted anemone (*Urticina lofotensis*), 39
white-spotted rose anemone (white-spotted anemone *Urticina lofotensis*), 39
white-streaked dirona (frosted nudibranch *Dirona albolineata*), 83
wide chink-shell (wide lacuna *Lacuna vincta*), 70
wide desmarestia (flat acid kelp *Desmarestia ligulata*), 160
wide lacuna (*Lacuna vincta*), 70
wild nori (laver *Porphyra* sp.), 169
window seaweed (sea lettuce *Ulva fenestrata*), 157
wine-glass hydroid (*Obelia* sp.), 28
winged kelp (*Alaria marginata*), 164
Winter Cove Provincial Marine Park, 196
wireweed (sargassum *Sargassum muticum*), 168
woody chiton (*Mopalia lignosa*), 56
worms: flatworms, 43; marine, 43–52; peanut, 43, 52; ribbon, 43, 44; segmented, 43, 45–52
wrinkled amphissa (*Amphissa columbiana*), 76
wrinkled dove snail (wrinkled amphissa *Amphissa columbiana*), 76
wrinkled purple (frilled dogwinkle *Nucella lamellosa*), 74
wrinkled seapump (warty tunicate *Pyura haustor*), 147
wrinkled whelk (frilled dogwinkle *Nucella lamellosa*), 74

X
Xanthoria candelaria (mealy sunburst lichen), 178

Xanthoria lychnea. See mealy sunburst lichen (*Xanthoria candelaria*)
Xiphister atropurpureus (black prickleback), 151

Y
Yakan Point, 190–91
yellow shore crab (*Hemigrapsus oregonensis*), 123
yellow-edged cadlina (yellow-edged nudibranch *Cadlina luteomarginata*), 80
yellow-edged nudibranch (*Cadlina luteomarginata*), 80

Z
Zirfaea pilsbryi (rough piddock), 100
Zirphaea pilsbryi (rough piddock), 100
Zostera sp. (eel-grass), 183

Other Outdoor, Science & Nature books from
HARBOUR PUBLISHING

WHALES OF THE WEST COAST
David A.E. Spalding

Here is a book that will answer every question you ever had about whales of the west coast. Includes information on whale watching, a west coast whale chronology, a calendar of whale events throughout the Pacific Northwest, and listings of museums, parks, hotlines, archives, research agencies and readings.
ISBN 1-55017-199-2 • 216 pages • 6 x 9 • 80 photos • $18.95 paper

WHELKS TO WHALES
Coastal Marine Life of the Pacific Northwest
Rick M. Harbo

This full-colour field guide to the marine life of coastal British Columbia, Alaska, Washington, Oregon and northern California is perfect for divers, boaters, beachwalkers and snorkellers of every experience level. Includes a glossary, checklist, reading list and full index.
ISBN 1-55017-183-6 • 248 pages • 5¹/₂ x 8¹/₂ • 512 colour photos • $24.95 paper

FIELD IDENTIFICATION OF
COASTAL JUVENILE SALMONIDS
W.R. Pollard, G.F. Hartman, C. Groot and Phil Edgell
Illustrations by C. Groot, photos by Phil Edgell

This important field guide is a must for biologists, resource assessment workers, forestry workers, salmon enhancement groups, naturalists, fisheries students and members of the public interested in fisheries projects.
ISBN 1-55017-167-4 • 32 pages • 5¹/₂ x 8¹/₂ • 15 colour photos & over 60 b&w and colour illustrations • Inside pocket with waterproof viewing bag • $12.95 paper